WILL YOU FIND THE POT OF GOLD
AT THE END OF THE RAINBOW?
THESE LUCKY FORTUNE-HUNTERS DID!

A Healthy Income
Over twenty years ago, Kay Modgling was advised by her doctors to exercise by taking a daily walk. She decided to bring along a metal detector. She has since found over 500,000 valuable items—and earned the name Queen of the Treasure Hunters.

Smokin' Stogies
A man in Ireland happened across boxes of cigars in the wine cellar of his nineteenth-century house. Experts informed him that the cigars are considered to be among the finest in the world. He has been offered $1 million for one box.

A Net Profit
A fisherman from Mobile, Alabama, snagged his net on some debris. The debris turned out to be the remains of *El Cazador*, a ship that sank in the Gulf of Mexico in the late 1700s, carrying a fortune in silver coins. Several hundreds of thousands of dollars' worth of silver has since been salvaged, and the effort is expected to continue for many months!

WHEREVER YOU LIVE,
WHATEVER YOUR LIFESTYLE . . .
YOUR TREASURE IS WAITING TO BE DISCOVERED!

THE HUNT FOR AMAZING TREASURES

Sondra Farrell Bazrod

A DELL TRADE PAPERBACK

A DELL TRADE PAPERBACK

Published by Dell Publishing
a division of Random House, Inc.
1540 Broadway
New York, New York 10036

Based upon the television series
The Hunt for Amazing Treasures
produced by and copyright © by Andrew Solt Productions
See photo credits: Pages 227–228.

Dell books may be purchased for business or promotional use or for special sales. For information please write to:
Special Markets Department, Random House, Inc.,
1540 Broadway, New York, NY 10036.

DTP and the colophon are trademarks of Random House, Inc.

LIBRARY OF CONGRESS CATALOGING IN PUBLICATION DATA
Bazrod, Sondra Farrell.
The hunt for amazing treasures / Sondra Farrell Bazrod.
p. cm.
ISBN 0-440-50888-6
1. Collectors and collecting. 2. Collectibles. I. Title.
AM231.B39 2000
790.1′ 32—dc21 99-23462
CIP

Printed in the United States of America

Published simultaneously in Canada

December 1999

10 9 8 7 6 5 4 3 2 1
BVG

Designed by Kathryn Parise

To Tux
A Real Treasure

ACKNOWLEDGMENTS

I would like to thank my children, Carla and Mark, for their continued support and inspiration. They are always treasures. Many thanks to my editor, Michael Shohl, for his heroic patience and perceptive editorial comments. A special thank-you to my agent, Giles Anderson, who made this book possible because he knows how material should be presented and works quickly and well. Many thanks to Andrew Solt Productions, and especially Andrew Solt for his decision to produce *The Hunt for Amazing Treasures.* It would not have been possible without his artistic guidance and the excellent work of the others associated with the program: Greg Vines, who originally took an interest in my ideas and encouraged me; and the other members of the production team, Marc Sachnoff, Joel Lippman, Dahlia Greer, Joan Owens, Ken Wiederhorn, Mary Sherwood, Danny Balber, Paul Lichtenberg, Tim Tobin, James Gallagher, Jr., Ray Wolf, Natasha Gjurokovic, Leslie Tong, Harvey Becker, and Gary Sommerstein. A special thanks to Steven Brattman, who also offered support and good advice. Thank you, Todd Schwartz, for making it happen.

INTRODUCTION

One person's treasure may be another person's junk. The word *treasure* usually fires the imagination with thoughts of sunken galleons full of gold and precious jewels waiting to be found. Whether the motivation is profit or pleasure, it's a fact that treasure hunting has become a way of life for many people looking for all sorts of things, from precious metals to bottles. Those who sell metal-detecting equipment, and the editors of treasure magazines, estimate that there are more than two million people of all ages enthusiastically looking for their pot of gold.

So many things can be called treasure. Some people search for relics of historic significance such as letters, weapons, furniture, and books. At any given time, thousands of intrepid investigators are out metal detecting at beaches, dredging rivers and streams for gold, digging in old dumps and ghost towns, or frequenting swap meets and garage sales.

The fascinating aspect of treasure is that people who were not particularly looking for it found items that appeared to have little value and then learned they had something worth a fortune. It happens more than one would imagine. In the following pages you will read about a diverse group of treasure hunters. Some set out specifically to follow their dream and find their object of wonder. Most of the people had no idea they had a treasure at home, in the garage or attic, until good fortune shined upon them.

In many instances, someone else told the owner of the "treasure" to check on the value. Then came the wonderful surprise that some have described as similar to winning the lottery. Treasures were found in the walls of a house, behind a disliked painting, under a couch, and in a school where students threw darts at something worth many millions of dollars.

In the annals of amazing treasure stories, it appears that people who save things have often reaped the rewards. This particularly applies to some papers found in an attic. What if the owner of the home had been on a neatness binge? It will make you shudder just to think of this treasure being thrown in the trash.

In addition to your reading about many different treasures, some you might not have thought of before, the aim of this book is to let you know that it can happen to you.

THE HUNT FOR AMAZING TREASURES

CHAPTER 1

The Huck Finn Manuscript

A Hollywood librarian knew she had to clean out the musty, cluttered attic of her lovely home on a quiet tree-lined street just minutes away from Paramount studios. It was fortunate that she had the attic in which to store the trunks and boxes that had been there for thirty years—not many southern California homes have attics and practically none have basements.

Mary, the name we'll use since she has preferred to remain anonymous, occasionally wondered about the contents of those six steamer trunks and boxes. Each time she thought of going through the containers she had inherited from her grandfather, though, she would sigh and, perhaps using Scarlett O'Hara's motto, would tell herself tomorrow was another day. After all, she had been raising four children and working full-time through the years. On each visit to the attic, whenever there was an extra lamp to store or a child's toy to keep, she would look at the ever growing assortment

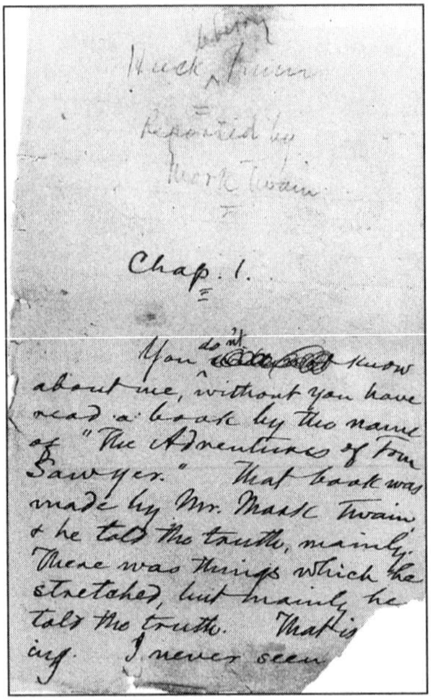

Huck Finn

Reported by
Mark Twain

Chap. 1.

You don't know about me, without you have read a book by the name of "The Adventures of Tom Sawyer." That book was made by Mr. Mark Twain & he told the truth, mainly. There was things which he stretched, but mainly he told the truth. That is ... I never seen

***A page from the original handwritten copy of Mark Twain's* Adventures of Huckleberry Finn.**

of mementos of her life and feel overwhelmed by the thought of organizing things.

One day while rummaging in the attic, she lifted the tray from one of the black, dusty, scratched steamer trunks and put it on an empty space of a shelf near the eighteen crammed bookshelves that covered one wall. As her hand went to the papers in the trunk tray, the phone rang, ending her attic adventure for the day.

Finally, during the Labor Day weekend in 1990, she knew the time had come. "I had three days and I knew I had to get to it," she said. "I went first to the tray of the old trunk I had put on the shelf and found a lot of what looked like thin sheets of paper that looked like there was handwriting on them, wrapped in a very frail piece of brown wrapping paper. It said Mark Twain Huck Finn MSS. I couldn't believe it at first, but there it was." As she scanned the hundreds of small, faint-blue-lined pages, she noticed that the first ones were written in black ink, and later ones in purple.

Mary first consulted the old college paperback of *The Adventures of Huckleberry Finn* that was nestled among the thousands of books in her home. "It had the same words, but the version I found had added passages and corrections and crossed-out words and sentences. There were scraps that had additions and revisions," she said.

Mary still found it hard to believe she'd found something so important. She held those fragile pages and compared them to the printed book. Her next step was the most logical. She went to the library and found a book with Twain's handwriting. "It was the same, so I thought, 'aha!' and then I called my sister who lives on the East Coast," Mary said. "She suggested we call Sotheby's in New York, and since she lived in the same time zone I told her to make the call." After her sister called Sotheby's, they asked to have copies of the first and last pages faxed to them, which Mary did. When the faxed pages arrived in New York, David Redden, executive vice-president, called the Beverly Hills office of Sotheby's and excitedly asked one of the document experts there to rush to Mary's home, because he believed the manuscript was the "real thing." The local expert confirmed the find and was thrilled to be touching those original pages of Huck Finn.

"It was so exciting," Mary remembers. "Sotheby's hired an armored truck to take the manuscript to the airport for its trip to New York Sotheby's after it was packed as though it were a precious gem, and of course it was." She added, "When I told my neighbor about it, she told me her mother would have thrown out everything in the attic long ago because she didn't believe in having clutter around. Fortunately, I don't think that way." The thought of throwing out such a treasure gave Mary chills. What a loss it would have been!

When the handwritten 665-page manuscript arrived in the hands of ebullient David Redden, he said, "This is a real treasure. These passages were never seen before. It really is an extraordinary story. After we received the call from California that there might be an original Huck Finn manuscript, I thought, 'my goodness, it's very doubtful,' but hope springs eternal and one of the lessons I try to teach everyone at Sotheby's is never to dismiss anyone who calls on the telephone. When we received the manuscript we were aghast. It clearly was the most extraordinary literary discovery of the postwar period."

The news spread around the country and also 400 miles north to the Buffalo and Erie County Library, which houses one of this country's largest Twain collections. In fact, the library had been guarding the typewritten second half of the original Huck Finn, which had been there since its publication in 1884.

Mary's grandfather, James Fraser Gluck, had been a trustee of the Buffalo and Erie County Library and loved to collect original manuscripts. He often corresponded with noted authors and asked them to send original copies of their writings after publication. Because Mark Twain had lived for a time in Buffalo and Gluck admired his work, he wrote to Twain, asking if he would send the original *Huckleberry Finn* manuscript to the library. Twain sent the typewritten second half to Gluck and told him the first half seemed to have been lost by the publisher.

Twain's letter said, "The first half was copied by the pen, and when the book was finally finished, the original of that half probably went to the printers and was destroyed." He added, "Half of the Finn book (second half) is extant because that half was written after the typewriter came into general use. Before that, it was my custom (and everybody's in my line, no doubt) to have my books copied with a pen and ship the original to the printers, who never returned it."

Twain was mistaken and is believed to have later found those first handwritten pages and sent them on to the Buffalo library. In a letter dated 1887, Gluck and another library official acknowledged receiving the first half of the manuscript.

When the first half of *Huckleberry Finn* arrived at the library, Gluck took it home to read it, as he usually did when manuscripts were received. He was only forty-five years old at the time, but he caught a cold that turned into pneumonia, and died within a few days. The distraught family packed many of his papers, never realizing that Huck Finn was among them. In the 1920s the family moved to southern California. When Gluck's wife died, one of their two daughters, Mary's aunt, inherited everything, and just kept the memorabilia in trunks and boxes. In 1961, the aunt died and the inheritance ended up in Mary's attic. There Huck Finn remained until that fateful day in 1990.

William H. Loos, the rare book curator of the Buffalo library, asserted their claim on the manuscript and the planned auction at Sotheby's was off. When he touched those precious frail pages, Loos was filled with emotion. "It was like a bolt from the blue," he said. "I was in a state of shock. It was something we had written off as not in existence." He said that the scores of revisions in Twain's hand gave insight to his thinking process as he created the Mississippi River tale. "There were whole paragraphs not in the published version. He rewrote the famous opening line three times, 'You will not know me . . .' he starts out. Then, 'you do not know about me . . .' and finally, 'You don't know about me, without you have read a book . . .' "

Mary says, "It would have been my grandfather's wish that the manuscript go to Buffalo. Any financial gain that might have come from the sale is not as important as making sure things are done right."

When Redden at Sotheby's was asked how much the manuscript was worth, he said, "It has to be worth over a million dollars or more. Who knows for sure."

In 1986 a box full of Twain letters, later appraised for half a million dollars, turned up in a hobby shop in Los Angeles. Twain's eldest daughter, Clara, had lived in Hollywood and once held a yard sale that disposed of her father's books and letters, although none compared to Huck Finn.

Poor Mark Twain, he had many tragedies in his life, especially concerning his children. Of his three daughters, two died while in their twenties, and Clara, the eldest, never had a good relationship with him. She felt he favored the other sisters, so she left home and traveled before marrying a Polish symphony conductor and musician, a man who turned out to be a compulsive gambler—which is why she continually had to sell anything of value that had belonged to her father.

Clara lived to be eighty-eight and died in the 1960s in San Diego, California, never knowing that in Hollywood, resting in Mary's attic, was the treasure, Huck Finn. Had she been able to get her hands on it, she certainly would have sold it to pay her debts.

Clara's only child, a daughter, grew up in Los Angeles and longed for a career as an actress. Unfortunately, she turned to drugs and alcohol. In 1964, while still in her early thirties, she committed suicide in an apartment on Highland Avenue in Hollywood, less than ten minutes away from Mary's attic, which had held her grandfather's masterpiece since 1961.

The manuscript made its final trip to Buffalo, and after seventeen months of meetings with attorneys and library officials, a confidential settlement was reached among the Gluck granddaughters, the library, and the Mark Twain Foundation. It was decided that any future royalties from the sale of the book to Random House would be divided equally. The new edition, published in 1997, has all the additions and changes that Mark Twain made in his handwritten pages but that are not in the original published version in 1884 and the reprints since then. The projection for royalties of the book is in the millions. Mary and her sister were delighted to find that their one third of the Random House advance was a real treasure financially and that they will receive a third of the future royalties.

Twain expert Victor Dyono said, "Now people can follow this work of art as it was changing on Mark Twain. It's a gold mine of information."

Daniel Mennaker, the Random House editor of the new version of *Huckleberry Finn,* said, "I felt as if some of the gold came my way. It's an editor's dream to disseminate new information and let the public see it." He adds, "Mark Twain is the best-selling fiction writer in the world. About one million copies a year are sold in sixty-five languages. There is only one original."

At the Buffalo library, Loos guards the treasure as though it were a precious jewel. It's kept in a vault in a stable environment and he brings out only a few pages at a time. "I wonder if I'm its keeper or if it's mine," he says. "To have the greatest literary manuscript of the great American novel is wonderful. This is certainly the greatest literary discovery of the twentieth century."

Redden summed it up when he said, "All of us at Sotheby's are treasure hunters and we live for these discoveries. We love them. When I heard this had been discovered in an attic in California, it seemed so utterly wonderful, such serendipity. I went to California and went up in that attic myself because I thought, 'well maybe *Hamlet, Macbeth, King Lear,* who knows what else could be there.' It just seemed too extraordinary, but I found an old Ping-Pong table and a broken lamp or two. This seemed to be it for that attic, but attics are wonderful places. They really are."

And Mary, whose attic had kept the priceless papers safe for all those years, could add only, "Yes, it was certainly enough treasure for one lifetime to find those handwritten words from the greatest American novel."

This leaves the rest of us to ponder the coincidences of life. What forces were at play to place this masterpiece of literature in the hands of a librarian?

CHAPTER 2

THE *MARAVILLA*

"Treasure is trouble. The more treasure the more trouble. The *Maravilla* was nothing but trouble. It's a cursed wreck." These are the words of Bob Marx, world-renowned underwater archaeologist and treasure hunter who has probably found and researched more sunken ships than anyone else alive. His quest to find the *Maravilla,* the second-richest Spanish galleon ever lost at sea, became an obsession and required a twelve-year search. The vessel was carrying 650 passengers and, according to the manifest, 5 million pesos of gold and silver, jewelry, emeralds, pearls, and other precious artifacts back to King Philip IV of Spain. Leading a fleet of ships, the *Maravilla* went down January 4, 1656, 30 miles off the coast of the Bahamas.

Marx's odyssey began when he ran away from his home in Pittsburgh, Pennsylvania, at thirteen to become a helmet diver, in the days when divers after treasure on sunken ships still wore a whole suit complete with heavy helmet. By age fifteen, he was in California. There, he started a group of free divers who didn't use the suit or helmet. Scuba equipment was not yet on the scene.

In 1950, when Marx met Jacques Cousteau and worked with him, scuba diving had just begun and he formed a diving group called the L.A. Neptunes. He was already a treasure fanatic when he made his first significant find in 1951, three hundred gold coins from the sunken *Winfield Scott* off Anacapa Island off the coast of southern California, about 70 miles north of Los Angeles. It was an 1852 gold rush ship on a voyage to bring the precious metal from San Francisco through the Panama Canal to eastern cities.

Marx joined the marines in 1951, became a diving instructor, and traveled around the world. While in the Mediterranean, he found gold and silver coins and other treasures on Greek, Roman, and ancient Phoenician wrecks.

He had met Mel Fisher, another future legend of the deep, in the early 1950s when Mel had the only compressor used for diving in his Redondo Beach, California, dive shop. In 1955 he and Fisher went to Cozumel, Mexico, to make a movie and found only about five hundred people living there—a far cry from the popular resort of today.

Marx stayed until 1959, finding what he describes as tons of treasure and starting the first diving resort and hotel. Hotel rates were $8 a day at first, a sum that would leave today's tourists in shock.

Marx says, "Mel Fisher became interested in treasure hunting around 1963 and we worked together on projects. We sometimes went to the American River and Sacramento River in the California gold country looking for gold nuggets." Fisher had not yet begun his search for the *Atocha,* a sunken Spanish galleon that would produce more than $400 million in treasure after he found it in 1985. Marx, however, was already obsessed by the *Maravilla.*

He had first read about the galleon in 1960 when fascination with sunken treasure took him to the Archive of the Indies in Seville, Spain. The Spanish had kept track of everything from the time of Columbus, and there were records describing the treasures that the heavily laden galleons were bringing home from the New World. Between 1552 and 1800, two thousand Spanish treasure galleons were lost at sea in the Western Hemisphere, but the only one Marx wanted was the *Maravilla.*

He made a number of trips to the archive and went through fifteen thousand documents for clues. One was a prayer written by a priest who survived:

Blessed by the light of the day
and the holy cross we say:
Blessed be the immortal soul
and the Lord who keeps it whole
Blessed by the light of day
And he who sends the night away

Legend said the *Maravilla* was cursed, and it appeared the curse had claimed her. She sank in 1656. Forty-five people survived the disaster and returned to Spain to tell the story. As thanks for their lives, some of the survivors donated money for the construction in Madrid of two churches, both named Maravilla, that still stand today.

Marx describes what happened after the fleet, led by the sleek *Maravilla,* left Havana Harbor, New Year's Day, 1656:

"For all the ships returning to Spain from the New World, the last stop was Havana and then up through the straits of Florida. They would try to spot what is now Cape Canaveral and then they knew they were far north enough to head for the northeast, Bermuda, the Azores, and home. The whole fleet turned to the northeast too soon. They didn't see the Cape but assumed they were far enough north, but were really 50 miles further south. It was a fatal mistake, a disaster.

"It was after midnight and all were asleep when a lookout realized they were in less than 20 feet of water off Little Bahama Bank. The captain ordered a cannon to be fired to warn the other ships and then all hell broke loose. One of the other ships hit the *Maravilla* on the side and put a large hole in it. The captain tried to keep everyone from drowning at once and tried to get the ship up higher on the bank but it hit a reef and broke into two pieces. The people knew they were going to drown but there was a little time so the priests who were on board charged two hundred pieces of eight coins for each person who wanted to make confession. The priests drowned first with their heavy treasure."

Marx says that although they were not far from land, many people in those days did not know how to swim. Even those who could had such heavy clothing it held them back. Over six hundred lost their lives while the lucky forty-five escaped the curse.

By 1968 Marx intensified his search for the elusive *Maravilla.* It came to be known as Marx's phantom wreck, but to him it wasn't a phantom and he believed he would find it. From the Spanish documents he knew he had 36,000 square miles of ocean to search, and while he was combing the bottom of the sea he saw sixty other ancient wrecks. When asked why the *Maravilla,* he knew the answer to that nagging question could be found in the middle of the Bermuda Triangle, where the mystical *Maravilla* had reached her final resting place.

Marx said, "You can find anchors with a magnetometer, a device that signals only iron when it is dragged by a ship along the ocean floor, but it doesn't signal treasure. Once you find an anchor or cannon you know there was a ship in the area. Through the years sand is deposited on top of any treasure that might be there. To find it you have to keep removing the overburden of sand on the bottom in various locations near the iron. Because we were in the Bermuda Triangle there were many times the magnetometers and radios wouldn't work." To add to the difficulties, they were plagued by sharks. On one occasion Marx received 268 stitches to close a shark bite. He said, "I guess the sharks didn't read my many books and articles stating that sharks don't bite!"

His optimism never wavered and he awoke every morning thinking it might be the day the *Maravilla* would be found. Finally it happened. August 24, 1972, was the climax of a twelve-year search. "After one of the magnetometer hits I suited up and went down for a look at what I expected to be the anchor," he said. "We had to blow about thirty feet of sand away and the first thing I found was a cannon ball. I took my hammer and knocked the core off and saw the English broad arrow mark which showed it was British property. Obviously, this was the wrong wreck, but something told me to remove the sand from a second spot and when I opened it there were thousands of silver and gold coins, jewelry and candlesticks. It was the *Maravilla.* We hit the Mother Lode!"

Marx also soon discovered that the main part of the *Mar-*

***Bob Marx with treasure recovered from the* Maravilla.**

avilla was 6 to 8 miles south and parts of the wreck were spread out over a 15,000-square-mile area. Many hurricanes over the years had moved the pieces and deposited 30 feet of sand on top.

One of the first items Marx found as he continued to retrieve treasure was an eighty-pound silver bar with the name of the ship's captain on it. "I like to bring history alive by finding things connected to people," he says.

Among the treasures for King Philip IV were porcelain bowls and other items from China. There were also smuggled pieces such as a twenty-five-pound solid gold bar with no markings. The regular gold bars were marked as twenty-one carats. Marx said, "There was always about 50 percent of the cargo in gold contraband being smuggled back."

As Marx retrieved more treasure, news traveled fast. Eleven times, ships with eager treasure hunters arrived upon the scene. To drive them away, Marx had to show that he had weapons aboard his recovery ship.

After six weeks, his ship was crammed with treasure and artifacts, and he arrived in the Bahamas, where he had an agreement with the government to share the treasure. However, the gossip that had preceded him said that his find was worth much more than it was, and he was greeted by armed guards. "The government said I was lying and banished me forever," he said. "It was the curse again!"

Marx could never return to the site, but he was the only one who knew exactly where it was. For fifteen years no one worked on the *Maravilla,* then he made arrangements with other divers. Since the early 1990s, Memphis-based Herbo Humphries and his company, Marex, have worked the wreck with their ship, the *Beacon.* They were not banned by the government of the Bahamas and have brought up millions in gold, jewels, and other artifacts, with Marx receiving a percentage of the profits. They and Marx estimate there are millions more yet to be found.

Several years ago, among many other valuables, Marex divers found an emerald and gold cross that was shown to the public when Cybill Shepherd wore it on the *Tonight* show with Jay Leno. It was later sold at auction for $550,000.

Marex divers are still at it, and Marx points out that amazing treasures, such as a life-size Madonna and child in solid gold, remain hidden in the sand.

"I've found multi-millions on the *Maravilla,*" Marx said, "but there were many debts to investors, the government of the Bahamas, and then Spain stepped in and I spent a fortune in court. It's been both a blessing and a curse. It will produce forever and ever."

In his fabled career Marx has worked in sixty-two countries and in 1995 went to thirteen different locations in the world. He has no plans to stop.

He says, "The thrill of discovery. It's in my blood."

Obviously, the one who wasn't cursed was the man, sometimes referred to as a priest, who survived the *Maravilla* and two other shipwrecks and returned to Spain to write about them. According to Marx's research, he actually was Diego Portichuelo de Ribadeneyra, head of the Spanish Inquisition for South America.

It does make one wonder!

CHAPTER 3

THE ASSYRIAN PANEL

Ancient art can show up in the strangest places. In this case, a three-thousand-year-old panel from the tomb of an Assyrian king was found in the sandwich shop of a private school in the south of England.

The Canford School in Dorset is surrounded by acres of lush green lawns and at first glance appears to be a country estate belonging to the very wealthy. In fact, that is what it was originally. Through the years, hungry students at the "Grubber" (the school sandwich shop, or tuck shop, as the commissary is called in England) paid little attention to the 4- by 6-foot whitewashed panel plastered into the wall. They thought it was the copy of something very old and occasionally threw darts at it, although they were more intent on playing the pinball machine nearby.

In 1993 the history of the panel was finally revealed, and

when it was put up for auction at Christie's in London, the hopes of the school went with it.

It all began in the mid-nineteenth century when Sir Henry Layard, a young man with an adventurous spirit, decided to go to India. He never went that far but stopped in Mesopotamia, which is now modern Iraq. He was a gregarious fellow, and he made friends there and listened to tales of the past. This led him to stumble across the ruins of the ancient Assyrian city of Nineveh, where he saw amazing artwork on stone panels. Layard felt he must bring some of these treasures back home, and was able to obtain a small grant from the British Museum. Then he faced the overwhelming problem of transporting the huge panels, which weighed up to forty tons. There was no machinery in those days, but merely ropes and pulleys. He dug for two years, 1847 to 1849, and was left exhausted and penniless after his museum grant ran out. Then he contracted malaria and went home to England. However, his work had produced many panels, which he was able to take with him.

Fortunately, his cousin Lady Charlotte Guest invited him to recuperate at her luxurious home, Canford Manor. Lady Charlotte was married to Sir John Guest, one of the richest men in England. It was not a marriage made in heaven, but one that was arranged. Sir John, twenty-six years older than his wife, had no title, but Lady Charlotte did.

Layard spent two months recuperating and was so grateful to his cousin that he offered her a gift of a group of the sculptures he had brought back from Nineveh. Even with such a huge home, Lady Charlotte felt she didn't have room for them, so she built what was referred to at the time as a porch. It really was the size of another house and afforded ample room for her to set the enormous panels into the walls.

When Layard and Lady Charlotte died, they were both buried near the estate. On Layard's grave it is noted that he was the discoverer of Nineveh. Lady Charlotte's grandson didn't like the sculptures, and sold them to pay estate taxes. In the 1920s, family heirs sold the manor house to a private school, which became the Canford School. The "porch" became the commissary, and no one remembered why it had been built. Everyone assumed that what they saw on the walls were some worthless plaster reproductions of the original sculptures.

Most of the original massive panels that Layard had given to his cousin ended up in the Metropolitan Museum of Art in New York City, a gift from John D. Rockefeller, Jr. He bought them from the man who had originally purchased them from Lady Charlotte's grandson. These sculptures were considered so important they were given their own gallery, which would undoubtedly have pleased Layard.

Around 1993, John Russell, a professor at Columbia University in New York City, was writing a book about the Canford sculptures and, having heard about the "porch," decided to visit the school in order to see where they had been and to take photographs for his book. First Russell went to the British Museum to do more research on the sculptures, and while there he happened upon what could be described as a treasure map of the "porch," which showed the exact locations of the various sculptures.

Russell describes what he saw when he went into the tuck shop. "Inside the door on the right wall were still some plaster casts and that was wonderful, but there was one I didn't

Assyrian panel, © Christie's Images, London

The Assyrian Panel, after being removed from the Canford School.

recognize. It wasn't a cast of a known piece." This was mystifying, so they scraped off the plaster and paint and Russell found underneath the type of marble that was used in the Assyrian sculptures. Through the years, no one had thought the sculptures were authentic, so whenever the walls were painted, the sculptures received an extra coat. Russell notified the school, and when the board of governors found they had an authentic ancient sculpture, they decided to have it sold at auction at Christie's in London.

John Lever, the headmaster, said, "It didn't look very special. How wrong we were. But once it was cleaned up you could see it far better and you do begin to stand and stare and wonder. It is a fairly remarkable thing now, but you can imagine covered in peeling paint it wasn't special at all."

The auction took place at Christie's on July 6, 1994. The school had been told the sale price might be about one million pounds. In just five minutes, the missing panel from the palace of the Assyrian king Ashurnasirpal II (883–59 B.C.) was sold for £7,701,500, or over $11 million, to an anonymous buyer from Japan. This made the panel the most valuable art antiquity ever discovered. Headmaster Lever summed up his and everyone at the school's feelings: "Absolutely astonished."

So the students who paid no attention to their unknown treasure will now have a new sports center, arts building, theater complex, refurbishing of the existing buildings, and a £2 million scholarship fund.

They can thank Sir Henry Layard, an absolutely astonishing treasure hunter.

CHAPTER 4

THE FAITH HEALER'S HOARD

A faith healer who didn't trust banks profoundly affected the life of a pharmacist who turned treasure hunter. Their lives intertwined in the Sierra foothills, 8 miles north of Placerville in northern California's gold country.

There, for a quarter century, all types of people had flocked to the timbered cabin of Francis Andre, the Goat Doctor of the Sierras. Many felt they were blessed and cured by the gentle, healing touch of the Goat Doctor, who was so named because of the flock of goats he cared for tenderly. However, the treasure hunter came to believe that not a blessing but possibly a curse was attached to the discoveries made on the property.

It began far away from California on July 20, 1888, in Vienna, where Francis Xavier Machek was born. His parents moved along with him to Czechoslovakia and died there when he was six years old. His relatives sent him to San

Francisco, where he lived with family friends until his early teens, when he began to support himself with wages from a job on a vegetable wagon. Perhaps it was fate that brought about his meeting with Elizabeth Andre, a clairvoyant who claimed to have exceptional intuitive powers, and her husband, Ernest, a poet and soldier of fortune. They were so taken with one another that the Andres adopted Francis and he took their name.

Because Andre was a sickly boy and his health deteriorated, his new parents took him to live in the cabin they built among towering fir and pine trees on the 75 acres of rugged and hilly land they bought near Placerville. In a 1957 interview in *The Sacramento Bee*, probably the only one he ever allowed, Andre said, "My mother knew there was only one thing to do for my condition. That was to get out in the hills and let God's healing powers work on me. After we came here, I began to recover. In the first few years I went around barefoot and naked, except for a loincloth. In those days . . . imagine . . . people around here called me 'the wild man.' I let my hair grow long because it's a conductor of electricity. If you cut it, it diminishes that power. It conducts the electricity from the air." He was convinced that the back-to-nature therapy saved his life.

He added, "Barefooted . . . don't forget that. You contact the soil directly and get the health giving powers of the good earth."

Though he had no formal training, Andre learned the healing arts from his mother, and continued to carry on her work after her death. He felt he had a sixth sense that enabled him, by the laying on of hands, to diagnose the exact ailment of his patient. There was, however, divided medical opinion about his ability. Some doctors thought of him as a self-taught chiropractor, whereas others said he achieved surprising success in certain cases. Most of the cases he treated were people with back problems. If he didn't think he could help someone, such as those with cancer and other ailments requiring medical treatment, he referred them to their family doctors.

Patients crowded the steep, winding narrow road to the Goat Doctor's cabin and were called in on a first-come, first-served basis. There was a flat $3 fee for all, preferably to be paid in silver. It was said that the wealthy and famous paid him much more in paper money because they were so grateful for his healing.

Beverly Cola of Placerville was treated by the Goat Doctor. She said, "He was really a different gentleman, very kind and soft-spoken, and soft-touching. It was a different experience, I'll tell you. People who went to him thought he could do no wrong, absolutely thought he could cure anything."

Erni McIneny, also of Placerville, added, "My mother had heard of him and since she had often used chiropractors, she decided to take me to him. There were cars parked along the road and people slept in them. The first time I saw him coming out of his house, his long hair was tied back and he was carrying buckets to take care of his goats. He was barefooted in overalls."

After his mother's death in 1949, Andre's father, who came to be known as the Poet Laureate of the Sierras, continued to live with him in the cabin. When Andre, a lifelong bachelor, married thirty-one-year-old Carmelita Munoz in 1957, on his sixty-ninth birthday, his father was ninety-one. His raven-haired bride had been Andre's barefoot assistant for five years after he cured her of what she said was a hopelessly crippling condition of her legs and back.

Alas, the couple had less than two years together before the Goat Doctor died on January 16, 1959, at age seventy. At that time his estate was valued at $74,500 in property and silver, of which the widow received $68,000, with the rest going to a relative of Andre's. This was not enough to pay all the taxes, and Carmelita lost the property and moved away. There had always been talk that the Goat Doctor would take paper money to the bank to exchange it for silver, which he would then take home to bury on his property. Gossip put the fortune at $750,000. Carmelita either couldn't find the treasure, or had chosen not to take it.

The Goat Doctor had already been healing people for fifteen years in 1930 when James Anthony Normandi was born July 20 on the family ranch in Petaluma, Sonoma County, California, not far away. That they both had the same birthday was just the first coincidence.

When Normandi was seven the family moved to Marin County, just across the bay from San Francisco, and there he grew up. In 1952 he received a bachelor of science degree in pharmacy from the University of California. In 1954 he returned from Korea after serving for two years as a first lieutenant in the medical service of the 7th Infantry Division. While in Korea he was fascinated by the bulky metal detectors the engineers used to clear minefields. He thought of other places where he could use detectors, and he remembered his childhood on the ranch, where he read *Treasure Island* and similar tales. Jimmy believed that the main charm of detecting involved touching the past and that using a metal detector could make dreams into reality.

Normandi settled in San Francisco and had to put treasure thoughts aside since he needed a job. After being hired as a pharmacist, he met a lovely young woman, Win, where he worked and soon they were married. His priorities now were to save for a house, not a costly metal detector. Soon there were three children, two sons, Tony and Jim, and a daughter, Angela, and in 1957 the family moved into their home in Marin County.

The thoughts of treasure were still with him, causing him to wander the hills and valleys of the Mother Lode with fishing rod in hand, poking at debris of ghost towns and mining camps. He knew it would be much more exciting to touch the hand of time by finding things underground, but he set that dream aside to open a pharmacy with a partner in 1963. The business was a success, but Normandi was a nervous wreck. Finally he bought a metal detector for relaxation. It wasn't a major brand and didn't work very well, but he loved it. Returning to the family ranch, he searched for the buried treasure his family had always discussed. He never found it but did find coins from the mid 1800s, which thrilled him.

One day Normandi read in the newspaper that a valuable gold coin had been found. He immediately called the finder to ask what type of detector he had used. When he was told it was a White's detector, he bought one, later saying, "I was beyond rescue." He spent every free hour with his precious detector, and his pile of coins and rings grew. His wife called it "Jimmy's Junk" and was delighted when he removed his treasures to the pharmacy, where he began selling White Metal Detectors. Since he drove the precious items there in his GMC Sierra, he called his business Jimmy Sierra Treasures and Jimmy Sierra, the name he continues to use, was born. The metal detector business in his pharmacy was a great success. He said, "I wasn't selling detectors. I was selling dreams, possible dreams."

Everyone knew it had to happen and it did. In 1979 Jimmy Sierra gave up the pharmacy and became a dealer for White Metal Detectors in San Rafael, California. His expertise in finding a variety of treasures grew, and people contracted with him to hunt for the items they believed would fulfill their dreams. Some were real, others merely illusion, but the searches took Normandi across the United States as well as to Mexico, England, and Scotland, where he often works with archaeologists recovering ancient coins and artifacts. He's quick to say, "The real treasure is in the search."

Was it destiny? Who knows? But in 1980 Jimmy Sierra first heard about the Goat Doctor of the Sierras and the Faith Healer's Hoard. They shared not only the same birthday but also the *Sierra* in their names.

It seems that a forest fire in 1979 had burned three structures on the Goat Doctor's property. Only the fireplace of the cabin where he had made his home was left. The current owner had hired two lumberjacks to clear the land because he had wanted to build a house there, but after the fire he decided to sell. Perhaps he thought there might be something to the legend of a curse.

As the men used a Caterpillar grader to clear burned debris near what had been a tack house for animals, they cut into the corner of a large chest underground. Suddenly, strewn over a 150-foot-long path they saw silver dollars and half-dollars and big rolls of silver certificates. Like a flash they began stuffing their clothes with the treasure, and eventually wound up filling three 5-gallon jerry cans. It was later estimated they had in excess of $50,000 market value.

The lumberjacks never showed up at their regular jobs again, but went immediately downtown and began spending the moldy $20 silver certificates and silver dollars in bars, which left them drunk for several days. Then they turned up in South Tahoe, Nevada, at the casinos, dropping those silver dollars at the blackjack tables.

Soon the rest of the lumber camp where the men had worked heard about the silver and little by little men disappeared from their jobs and reappeared on the Goat Doctor's property. One seeker realized a metal detector would be better than merely their shovels and picks, so he went to rent a detector from one of Jimmy Sierra's dealers, telling him coins were so plentiful that they were sticking to men's boots as they trudged through the mud. The man didn't divulge the exact location, but the dealer had lived in the area and from the bits of information figured out it was the Goat Doctor's land and drove there to see for himself. He found that other people had been digging and the area looked like a war zone. He also learned that at least four caches had been found and believed there would be more.

When he told Jimmy Sierra the story, Jimmy decided the best thing to do would be to get a contract with the current owner and sign a search-and-recovery agreement and split the find. The owner had been plagued by so many people on the property, he didn't want to hear the word *treasure,* but finally, nearly a year later, he agreed that Jimmy could spend a short time on the Goat Doctor's land. When Jimmy finally began his search, trusty metal detector in hand, it was the misty, rainy afternoon of Halloween in 1980.

Jimmy Sierra displays some of the coins from the Faith Healer's Hoard.

He says, "I went to a large pine tree in the center of the property. It was one of hundreds there. I had a funny feeling when I approached it. In fact the hair stood up on the back of my neck. I started to turn away. I immediately turned back, and with a feeling of supreme confidence, continued my search. As I walked slowly, I got an extremely strong signal with the metal detector."

He began to dig and one and a half feet down he hit the top of a rotted-out bank bag. "I could see the coins just bubbling out like a pomegranate breaking open. The coins went right to the roots and it took one and one half hours to retrieve 2,200 silver coins weighing about forty pounds. It was a thrill. I'll never forget it."

Before Jimmy had a chance to continue the search, the owner said he had to leave and Jimmy must also go. It was already getting dark, so Jimmy had no choice. He and the owner finally divided the find, but the owner canceled the contract for any future hunts.

The following February, Jimmy's share of the Goat Doctor's silver was stolen from his metal detector showroom, where it had been proudly displayed. The value of the coins was about $10,000. He says, "People talked about a curse and I began to take it seriously."

The lure of the Goat Doctor's treasure was strong, and a year later, again on Halloween, Jimmy went back to the property after making an arrangement with yet another owner. This time he went to the old orchard area and had that same feeling that something was there. He found two large cans of silver dollars amounting to about $10,000.

The next day, with the help of a bulldozer, Jimmy found a large money box containing paper money, silver certificates, and silver. The total of Jimmy's various searches had provided nearly $40,000 in silver as well as heartache mixed with exhilaration. In 1995, Jimmy again returned to the Goat Doctor's land. There was now another owner, who was definitely skeptical about talk of treasure but finally agreed to a search. Jimmy says, "I had stayed away for many years and had mixed feelings about going back, but once there all the old feelings came back. It was a misty, rainy day, same as that original day. I took a while to locate the tree but once I did I had the feeling I should do it again. I went down by the fireplace and a minute into it found a silver half-dollar."

Because the weather turned bad, they couldn't continue, but the find made a believer out of the owner.

Treasure is still being unearthed, but Jimmy has never returned. At least $100,000 has been found. How much more is there? Who knows?

Jimmy later learned that the third coincidence between him and the Goat Doctor was that his father was born the same year as the Goat Doctor and died around the same time.

In his ongoing quest to find treasure that will provide a glimpse of history, Jimmy Sierra takes several trips to England each summer, leading groups of people from all walks of life who also have been dreaming of finding that special artifact they can hold in their hands and know they are now truly treasure hunters. The tours have been successful and are conducted with the cooperation of the British government, which has strict laws concerning the finding of treasure.

Though the Goat Doctor treasure so affected Jimmy, he says that there is one way he wants to be remembered. "I want to be known for encouraging other people to follow their imagination and begin the journey to make their dreams come true."

CHAPTER 5

El Cazador

It was at their home in Grand Bay, Alabama, on an evening in mid-July 1993 that Myrna Reahard said to her husband, James, a commercial fisherman, "It would be wonderful to find a treasure. I wonder what it would be like if such a thing happened to us."

She had no idea how prophetic her words were or how soon it would come to pass.

Two weeks later, on August 2, Reahard's nephew, Jerry Murphy, who worked with him, was out in the Gulf of Mexico trawling for butterfish in the company's boat, the *Mistake.* They didn't know until they brought the net up and saw a tear in it that it had caught on what seemed to be some rocks on the bottom. The rocks in the net appeared to be round, but a crew member looked at them carefully and realized they were silver coins. There were a thousand coins in the net. Murphy carefully noted the boat's exact location and called his uncle when he returned to land.

It was just after dinner when Reahard heard Murphy say that he had good news and bad news. The bad news was, he had torn up a $10,000 net, but the good news was that he probably made the best drag of his life. The catch was hundreds of silver coins dated 1783.

According to the journal Myrna Reahard began keeping as soon as they heard the news, she and her husband laughed and giggled and danced a little jig around the table and then decided they needed a lawyer.

They contacted their friend David Paul Horan in Key West, who represents most of the modern-day treasure salvors in the United States. He is best known for having successfully prosecuted Mel Fisher's claim to the 1622 Spanish galleon *Nuestra Señora de Atocha.*

When the Reahards told Horan every coin was dated 1783 and marked "Carolus III," he told them it had to be a shipment from a mint. He also informed them that a salvage claim needed to be filed and warned that deep-water salvage was very expensive. The then unknown ship was 300 feet down.

The next order of business was to hire Robert Stenuit, Belgian researcher in maritime history and consultant in nautical archaeology, to determine what ship they had found. He went to the Archive of the Indies in Seville, Spain, where every ship and cargo was meticulously noted. After his research he said the ship had to be *El Cazador,* a two-masted square-rigged Spanish brig bringing coins from the Spanish mint in Vera Cruz, Mexico, to Louisiana, which was owned by the Spanish in 1784. King Carlos III was on the throne, thus the marking "Carolus III" on the coins.

On January 11, 1784, *El Cazador* left Vera Cruz with a cargo described in the manifest as 400,000 pieces of eight, which were freshly minted in 1783 at the mint in Mexico City. In addition there were 50,000 other coins of various denominations. The mission of the ship was to bring hard currency to Spanish Louisiana and New Orleans. The coins were needed to redeem discredited Spanish paper money that was put in circulation after the Spanish took the Louisiana Territory from France in 1763.

After leaving Vera Cruz, *El Cazador* disappeared without a trace. Its loss had an effect on history. The Spanish paper currency being circulated in New Orleans and Louisiana continued to be discredited, and negotiations between the Spanish and Napoleon culminated in the trade of Louisiana and New Orleans to the French in 1800. Three years later, Napoleon sold New Orleans and Louisiana to President Thomas Jefferson for $15 million. Perhaps none of this would have happened if the money on *El Cazador* had reached its destination.

The Reahards, Jerry Murphy, and some others involved in the find formed the "Grumpy Partnership" and filed a salvage action in the United States District Court in New Orleans. They were represented by Horan, who pointed out that since the wreck site was in international waters there could be problems. "Every major treasure find during this century has been extensively litigated by either state or federal government, insurance companies, etc. It is my hope that this major find will be adjudicated without any adverse claims being filed." He got his wish. The Grumpy Partnership became owners of *El Cazador* and were ready to proceed with salvage. That's when the problems began, and Myrna Reahard soon had an

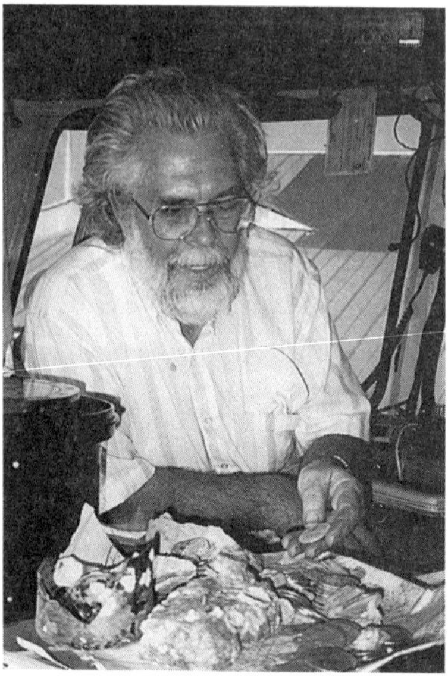

***Captain Jerry Murphy inspecting treasure from* El Cazador.**

answer to the question she had asked before the treasure appeared: "I wonder what it would be like if something like that happened to us?"

The first company to work on the salvage was Marex, headed by Herbo Humphries of Memphis, Tennessee. They had previously successfully salvaged other sunken ship's treasures including finding millions in jewels and gold on the Spanish galleon *Maravilla,* which went down in 1656 off the Bahamas. Coins were salvaged from *El Cazador,* but things did not go as planned, and there were problems with equipment because of the 300-foot depth. Problems mounted as some investors wanted out while others wanted in.

Mrs. Reahard's journal became a newsletter for all those involved with the treasure. In mid-October 1993 she noted: "This letter should be full of wonderful news about silver coins and artifacts. None of you can be more disappointed than me that this is not the case. We have spent most of three weeks trying desperately to iron out all the wrinkles with investors, salvage people and attorneys. About the time we think we have all the wrinkles out, a new one pops up! It has been very frustrating."

The next company to work on the salvage was Oceaneering, based in Louisiana. They had expertise in deep-water work and used a specially designed suit called the Wasp as well as a one-man submersible. They eventually brought up several tons of coins but were also plagued by the equipment problems that are quite common in this type of work. Finally, Oceaneering had to go back to their oil contracts, the primary source of their business.

The partners learned that Horan had been right when he warned that underwater salvage was expensive. The costs ran from $25,000 to $40,000 per day. Even though five and a half tons of silver coins were salvaged, Reahard wondered, "Are we going to be able to make it?"

Because a number of treasure ships bearing coins have been found in recent years, the numismatic value, which pertains to coin collectors and dealers, is not as high as it once was. The Reahards have three hundred thousand coins, mostly in a vault, though some have been sold to dealers and collectors, there is much yet to be done to reap the rewards of finding a treasure.

They learned that they had to become treasure marketers and make up certificates for all the coins to be sold. Reahard says, "The price of the coins is based upon their condition and they range from $29 to $300." He adds that there are gold coins among the silver that are very valuable, and some of the silver coins are dated 1732 and every year thereafter. Many of the coins are still in clumps and need to be cleaned. He says, "We still don't know what we've got and no telling what it will be worth." If the coins are valued only at the price of silver per ounce ($5.50 in early 1999), the total would be more than a million dollars, but it will be quite a while before the true value is known.

Reahard has some theories on why *El Cazador* went down. He thinks the ship burned. "We can tell by the state of the wood and the fact that utensils are broken. Fire would have caused that to happen." He adds that iron was carried on ships, and they also had a forge to work with the iron. There was a place to build a fire that would be protected so sparks could not fly out, but bad weather could have caused one coal to get too near the wood and ignite.

Reahard suspects that it was probably an El Niño year because there were many hurricanes and they were much later than usual. In the research it is noted that the captain was going to "wait on the moon" until October so he would miss the hurricane season, but luck and weather were not with him.

In March 1996 the Reahards opened a museum in Grand Bay, Alabama, and proudly display coins and artifacts from their amazing treasure. James believes *El Cazador* did change the course of history, which makes the discovery of the ship so important to him. "Had they made it back, Spain would have kept control of Louisiana, perhaps Mexico and the southern part of the United States and there might never have been the Louisiana Purchase. These coins have a story to tell."

Meanwhile, Reahard and his partners continue their fishing business. "It's our hope that we'll get enough monetary reward from the treasure that there will be enough for everyone to retire one day," Reahard says, "but even if not, it is an experience that most people never even dream of in their lifetime."

CHAPTER 6

MOVIE POSTERS

It was 1992 when Bill Moorehouse and Joseph Foxhood bought a Victorian house built in 1909 in Three Oaks, Michigan. They knew the roof was bad, but were optimistic that it would hold up until they could afford to repair it. Little did they know that the walls were literally stuffed with treasure and that Bill would soon exclaim, "It was like a dream come true. It was like winning the lottery."

The whole house needed remodeling, but it was a good deal and one they couldn't resist for an important reason: Foxhood had been living in his primitive farmhouse on his 23-acre property. It had no heat, and he was fed up with being cold.

Moorehouse, a furniture designer with a firm at the Merchandise Mart in Chicago, and Foxhood, a computer programmer for Shepherd's Hardware Products in Three Oaks, were also in the antiques business. They had previously bought and sold houses after refurbishing them.

The Victorian house bought by Bill Moorehouse and Joseph Foxhood.

Mother Nature didn't go along with their plans. A week after they moved into their new home, a big storm hit and, though they didn't have the money, they had to call the roofers and worry about paying the bill later. As the repairmen were tearing down some of the dampened plaster walls, they suddenly began finding inside them large poster-like cards placed five and six deep. They didn't know what they were but soon discovered they were window cards, which were smaller than movie posters but with the same pictures on them promoting films.

Moorehouse contacted dealers and described their find, prompting interested parties to fly in from various parts of the country. All were amazed to find that the window cards were more valuable than expected because they were from the early thirties and almost impossible to find. They learned that a former owner of the house had been the manager of the local movie theater during the Depression, and had brought home seven different cards each day to be used for insulation. Their size was just right to fit between the studs.

Dwight Cleveland of Chicago, a noted movie poster dealer, delighted in helping them rip down more walls when he arrived and was ecstatic at the treasures of Hollywood in the 1930s. He said, "These cards were entombed in the walls for sixty years and their condition was so good it was like they were in a time capsule."

There were thousands of posters found. Cleveland said, "There is an entire genre of film in one image. For example, *Footlight Parade* defines a whole generation of film and art and this card is worth between ten and fifteen thousand dollars." This prompted Moorehouse to say, "All this paper . . . old paper and it's worth money. It was really exciting." Some of the cards were for *I'm No Angel,* starring Mae West, *Song of Songs,* starring Marlene Dietrich, *Arizonian,* starring Richard Dix, and many of Busby Berkeley's films. Cleveland was particularly excited by *The Girl from 10th Avenue,* which had the picture of its star, Bette Davis, in a seductive pose. He said, "This is the only image of her as the sex goddess. There is no other known poster like this." He estimated that card to be worth around $8,500. Cleveland added, "This is the largest collection of posters ever found in one place."

So what did Moorehouse and Foxhood do next? They had to hurry to pay those roofers, so they sold most of the posters to dealers, including Cleveland, who purchased about five thousand. He said that over time, the posters would be worth hundreds of thousands of dollars. For a while Moorehouse and Foxhood kept twelve, including the Bette Davis and, of course, the one from the film *We're in the Money.*

They also used some of the money to put a down payment on a house they really wanted in Michigan City, Indiana, and moved there in 1993. Moorehouse had always longed to visit England, so their windfall allowed them to make the trip. Foxhood said, "The trip was very special to him. He had wanted to see the chrysanthemums in bloom in London and he did."

Tragically, in 1995, after just two years in their new home, Moorehouse passed away. Foxhood is grateful that the movie posters were able to make his dream come true. He says, "The treasure was Bill's baby. He took care of it all. It was a big learning experience for both of us."

Foxhood continues to live in the house and has found a small Prohibition era treasure in the cellar. "The mayor once owned the house, which was built around 1926. There's a little vault with an upright brick that said pull so I did and found a bottle of gin and Scotch with the original wax seal intact."

Foxhood now has just one poster left, *Break of Hearts,* starring Katharine Hepburn, his favorite actress. He says, "I had to keep something to remind me of all that fun."

CHAPTER 7

IRISH CIGARS

Cigars are all the rage these days and no more so than in the Grand Havana Room in Beverly Hills, California, a private club where many movie stars own humidors that keep their expensive brands in perfect condition. Though he has smoked the best, the co-owner and noted cigar connoisseur, Joe Pantoliano, sampled a rare cigar one day in 1996 and exclaimed, "I've been waiting my whole life for this cigar."

That cigar, estimated value $2,000, wasn't from Cuba or surrounding areas but had been, of all places, in the musty wine cellar of a ninety-seven-room manor constructed in 1864 called Temple House, a thousand-acre estate in Ballymote, Ireland. Lord of the manor Sandy Perceval also has the ruins of a thirteenth-century castle on his property, as well as a two-thousand-year-old fort.

Perceval says, "This area was populated from seven to ten thousand years ago. The castle was built in 1171 by the

Knights Templar and they moved in around 1200. That's how our home came to be called Temple House." He proudly notes that one of his ancestors, Perseval, was one of the Knights of the Round Table.

Amid all this history and lovely green rolling hills, Perceval raises 1,600 sheep. Temple House has been recognized by noted travel guides as an outstanding country house accommodation in the Emerald Isle. Through the years family friends and guests at Temple House had the pleasure of smoking excellent cigars that Perceval had found in boxes in the cellar when, in 1965, he actually began living in the house his family had owned for hundreds of years. Perceval had always enjoyed the cigars but didn't think much about their history until, one day in 1995, a friend smoked one and was so impressed and excited, he asked if he could take some to London to determine their true value. He also took a paper rubbing from the cigar box lid that could help determine the cigars' origin.

Perceval's great-great-grandfather Alexander, who was also known as "the Chinaman" because of his work as a prestigious barrister in Hong Kong, in 1864 loaded a ship with goods to sell, including the cigars, and sailed from the Orient home to Ireland. Those cigars had been rolled in 1864 while Abraham Lincoln was president and Queen Victoria was on the throne of England.

They were smoked on special occasions until Alexander died of a stroke three years later and his daughter-in-law Charlotte, an antismoker, banished them to the cellar. "She saved them from being smoked up altogether," Perceval said.

The word soon came from the friend that he had been correct about the value of the cigars and that there was an offer of $1 million from an American investor for an intact box of five hundred of what seemed to be the oldest cigars in the world. That would make each cigar worth $2,000. As a comparison, at a Davidoff cigar store in London a good Cuban cigar sells for between $9 and $30.

"I was astonished," Perceval said. "I never expected such a thing. When I grew up and my parents moved into Temple House they burned two or three thousand cheroot cigars they found in sacks. Those still in boxes were like a treasure chest left behind for heirs."

Suddenly, just when they needed them, the Percevals couldn't find an intact box of five hundred. They spent days scouring all those rooms. Finally, Mrs. Perceval found in a small wine cellar the last intact box. Thanks to the mist from a nearby lake, the Irish damp, and the temperature in the wine cellar, the cigars, just as the others had been, were in perfect condition in their own natural humidor.

There was a story about the cigars on the front page of *The Wall Street Journal* and network news programs in the United States and other countries. The cigar industry was abuzz with the news. Perceval said, "We could certainly use the money. There's been a slump in the sheep market and we needed to mend the roof, rejuvenate the house, and take care of inheritance taxes and health problems."

Before the cigars could be sold for the best price, Perceval had to prove where they were rolled. It was difficult to positively make out the markings on the embossed lid of the box, but the date was clearly written: they were made June 25, 1864, and they could also see the word *Manilla,* which could have been a brand name and not a location. Perceval sent the lid to Havana, Cuba, because that would have been the preferred place of origin. After waiting patiently for six months, the lid was returned with the information that the cigars were not Cuban. On one side of the crest were the faint letters FI and on the other side AS. It was thought this perhaps meant the cigars were made in the Philippines, which has also been spelled Fillipinas.

This would still mean the cigars were valuable because the Philippines had produced outstanding ones. Tobacco was not used in Europe until Columbus brought it back after landing in Cuba in November 1492 and observing natives smoking objects that looked much like modern cigars. Smoking caught on in Spain but was not as popular in other countries. It was said that Queen Elizabeth I didn't approve of smoking and kept tobacco from being widely used in England during her reign. Since Spain had owned the Philippines at the time the cigars were rolled, it would make sense that they could have been made there.

Perceval has become a super sleuth in his quest to discover the origin of the cigars. At one point he decided to have a cigar sent to Los Angeles so an expert could comment on it, but even this endeavor took a difficult turn. Perceval carefully packed the precious item in a small box and confidently sent it to Los Angeles via overnight courier service because Pantoliano at the Grand Havana Room had only a few days available to sample it. The cigar arrived the next day but was stopped at customs. Perceval would receive daily calls from representatives who said they had to positively identify what it was before they could clear it. The first question that was always asked was, "Is it food?" He would answer, "No, it's not food, it's a cigar. That's how it's marked."

Sandy Perceval proudly displays a box of rare cigars.

Then he would be told, "We'll get back to you." He continued to point out that the cigar was needed immediately but the pleas didn't help. He couldn't seem to get that 132-year-old cigar through customs. It probably had an easier time going from Hong Kong to Ireland in 1864 than it did getting through U.S. Customs to Los Angeles.

Finally, after several more days and calls asking, "Is it food?" someone decided how to classify that valuable, lonely, cotton-wrapped cigar. Perceval never learned how it was categorized, but it was rushed to the Grand Havana Room in Beverly Hills, where Pantoliano was ready. When a *Los Angeles Times* editor heard about the cigar, rather at the last minute, he tried in vain to get a reporter to the smoking test. The cigar was definitely reaching star status.

Pantoliano took his time to comment after he lit up and took his first puffs. "It's amazing how well it's been kept," he said. "It's pretty good . . . really good. It's a real spicy taste. It's fascinating that the ash is white. It's an interesting shape. Narrow at the end. It's difficult to make this way." Then he became more excited. "It's one of the better cigars I've ever smoked. Really terrific." Then the full impact hit him. "It's phenomenal. How many people get to smoke something this old. It should be $4,000 for each."

Perceval is now smoking the seconds and keeping the box of five hundred intact. "The main thing about all of them is they are slightly sweet and very cool," he says. "The modern cigars are warmer to smoke."

Hopefully, he will soon learn if the *Manilla* noted on the lid does mean the cigars were made in the Philippines. Several financial publications in Europe have recently written about the thriving cigar-making business now being carried on there. Then the Percevals will need to decide what to do with the box when they finally sell or auction the cigars. Should they sell the whole box or break them up? Mrs. Perceval would hate to see them broken up. A Dutch company, among others, is interested.

No matter what happens concerning the sale of the cigars, Perceval and his lovely wife, Deb, believe their home is their true treasure. He says, "Who knows what the next generation will find?"

CHAPTER 8

THE DECLARATION OF INDEPENDENCE

Some people scoff at the idea of finding anything worthwhile at flea markets, swap meets, and garage sales. In 1989 a man who fortunately didn't share that opinion went to a flea market in Adamstown, Pennsylvania, outside Philadelphia, and found the bargain of a lifetime.

The man we will call John, since he prefers to remain anonymous, looked over the items displayed and found a gilded and ornately carved picture frame that he liked. He had no interest in the picture it held, one he later described as a dismal, dark country scene with a signature he couldn't make out. Since the price was right, at $4, he bought the picture and frame.

When he arrived at home and began to remove the picture, the frame fell to pieces and he thought he had wasted his money. Then a document behind the picture fell out, folded about the size of a business envelope. John realized it

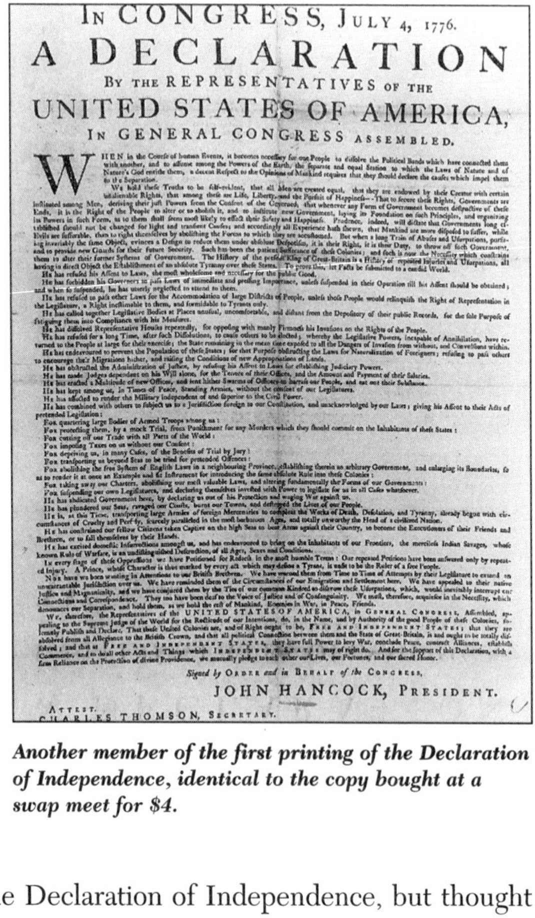
IN CONGRESS, JULY 4, 1776.

A DECLARATION

BY THE REPRESENTATIVES OF THE

UNITED STATES OF AMERICA,

IN GENERAL CONGRESS ASSEMBLED.

Signed by ORDER and in BEHALF of the CONGRESS,

JOHN HANCOCK, PRESIDENT.

ATTEST.
CHARLES THOMSON, SECRETARY.

Another member of the first printing of the Declaration of Independence, identical to the copy bought at a swap meet for $4.

was the Declaration of Independence, but thought it must be a copy printed much later, perhaps for the Bicentennial. He decided it was worth keeping and put it in a drawer. Two years later he showed it to a friend, who urged him to contact experts who could determine the true value. John then contacted Sotheby's in New York.

David Redden, executive vice-president and rare document expert at Sotheby's, said that John had a first printing of the Declaration of Independence. "It was in the most remarkable and wonderful condition," Redden said. "The first printing of the Declaration of Independence is the most important single page of printing in the history of the world. What happened is that on July 4, 1776, the Continental Congress declared independence and in order to disseminate the information they ordered the printer for the Congress, on the night of July 4, to print up the Declaration as the official Proclamation of Independence."

Of course, the fascinating and unsolved mystery will also be where John's precious page came from and why it was hidden behind that picture. At the time of its printing, a person caught with the Declaration could have been imprisoned.

Redden explained that several hundred were produced that night by the printer, John Dunlap, but to his knowledge only twenty-four, including this find, are known to have survived, and this copy was one of only three remaining in private hands.

The next order of business was to schedule an auction at Sotheby's, which was held on June 13, 1991, with David Redden as auctioneer.

"You never know what will happen at an auction," he said. The excited owner was in the audience, completely anonymous. Redden describes what happened. "We started at four hundred thousand and then the bidding got to eight hundred thousand and the owner looked relieved as though he thought it was now all over."

The bids slowly worked their way up and didn't stop when the figure reached $1 million. Redden said, "When the final figure of $2,200,000 ($2,420,000 with commission) arrived and I hit the gavel, the room erupted. The owner went away completely stunned. I think it took him six months to get over it."

The delighted buyer, Donald J. Scheer, said, "I think it's a bargain, particularly with what's going on in the world today. I think it's a living document. The words in this document are the words that knocked down the Berlin Wall and freed Poland."

When he purchased the Declaration of Independence, Sheer of Atlanta, Georgia, was president of Visual Equities Inc., a fine arts investment firm. He told the reporters who mobbed him that his firm had been prepared to pay considerably more.

Redden said, "I think it was just wonderful. Every time you find something like this it's so important because this is so integral to our history and not just our history but the history of the world. To find another copy of the first printing of the Declaration of Independence is a truly extraordinary find."

Since not all the copies of that first printing have been found there is hope that the others will turn up, probably in unexpected places. At least this Declaration remained near Philadelphia, the place of its origin, but the others could have traveled far afield and one might be tucked away in an attic in Alaska.

If you think you might have one of the first copies of the Declaration of Independence, remember, it has no signatures on it because those first pages with the memorable words of Thomas Jefferson were printed to notify all the states and were not meant to be signed. The first public proclamation of the Declaration was in Philadelphia on July 8, and then it was read before George Washington and his troops in New York City the next day. The Continental Congress resolved on July 19 to have the Unanimous Declaration copied on parchment for the signatures of the delegates. Most of the fifty-five signed on August 2, but one, Matthew Thornton, who was not a member of Congress when the Declaration was adopted, signed his name in November.

Perhaps you will now think differently when you pass a swap meet or flea market. Remember, one person's junk can be another person's treasure!

CHAPTER 9

THE MALTESE FALCON

Things that are shrouded in mystery seem to remain that way. Take the case of the Maltese Falcon, the star of Dashiell Hammett's classic novel and then the 1941 film starring Humphrey Bogart as Sam Spade, which many describe as one of the greatest detective movies of all time. It was John Huston's directorial debut. In the film, as in the book, everyone is looking for the statue of the golden bird encrusted with jewels that for six hundred years had carried the mystery of wealth and murder. When found, it turns out to be a fake made of lead.

In typical Hollywood fashion, after the movie was finished the prop disappeared and became a treasure even more sought after than the bird in the story. There were many fakes through the years, and the hunt was so popular that clubs were formed for the sole purpose of searching for the real thing.

Then the mystery appeared solved when Dr. Gary Milan, a retired dentist and avid collector, became the owner of the authentic Maltese Falcon because of his love for the film *Casablanca.*

He said, "I began collecting at eight and my mom thought I was crazy because I collected so many things such as letters, manuscripts, Revolutionary War and Hollywood items and more."

Around 1983, Milan went to an auction of items from a movie prop house and bought what was purported to be the piano from the Paris flashback scene in *Casablanca.* He wasn't certain it really was the piano because it had so many layers of paint on top of the original finish, but after stripping them away he knew it was "the" piano. This later enabled him to find the piano used in the scenes at Rick's Café Américain. Milan decided to put the flashback-scene piano up for auction at Sotheby's, and in 1988 it was purchased by a resident of the Orient for $154,000. Milan believes the piano would be worth a lot more at this time. He did not sell the piano from Rick's place because it played a far more important role in the film and he plans to keep it. He points out that throughout the movie it was in the Rick's Café Américain piano that the transit papers were hidden.

Milan said, "The Maltese Falcon was a serendipitous find. A wonderful treasure that when I purchased it I wasn't even certain it was the Maltese Falcon." Because of the publicity surrounding the auction of *Casablanca*'s Paris flashback-scene piano, Milan received a call from a man who told him he had "the" Maltese Falcon. Milan had previously seen 250 imitation and fake Maltese Falcons, so he asked the man why he thought it was the real thing. The caller responded that he thought it was right because it was lead and very heavy.

Milan said, "I went to see it and there, lying in a box, was 'the' Maltese Falcon." But he still wasn't absolutely certain, so he did extensive research at Warner Bros. Archives and uncovered original correspondence and memos relating to the film.

The Maltese Falcon, from the collection of Dr. Gary Milan. Maltese Falcon from the 1941 Warner Bros./Turner Entertainment Co. motion picture

***The statue for the falcon from the movie* The Maltese Falcon.**

For further information he consulted Hollywood memorabilia expert Charles Sachs, who had done the original appraisal of the Warner Bros. Archives. "This gave us a trail to follow," Sachs said. "Furthermore, the archive memos revealed its weight which was almost fifty pounds. John Huston was a stickler for accuracy and he called for a lead bird of significant weight as Hammett had described it in the novel. In one or more scenes you can actually see Bogart grimace when he picks up the bird and later walks downstairs very gingerly, tucking the bird to his chest and leaning back slightly so you know he's carrying something very heavy." Milan found a Warner Bros.' office communication stating that during one of the rehearsals Bogart dropped it and almost broke his toe, probably bending one of the bird's tail feathers.

The bird that Milan possessed weighed almost fifty pounds and had a bent tail feather. Sachs and Milan found photos taken from the film, showing the bent tail feather on one side, and features that matched Milan's "bird" exactly. They knew they had the real Maltese Falcon as seen on the screen, a fact confirmed by the Warner Bros. archivist at the Warner Bros. Museum. For years it was thought the one Milan bought was the only one known.

When Warner Bros. was preparing their museum, a prop man from *The Maltese Falcon* was interviewed and said there were two falcons. Because of their weight they were used as barbells by members of the crew.

Shortly afterward, this second bird surfaced and was put up for auction at Christie's in New York. Its owner at first had no idea she had the coveted prop because it had been given to her husband by Jack Warner. He put it on a shelf in a TV room where no one paid attention to it.

Nancy Valentino, consultant in entertainment memorabilia at Christie's, received a call one day from the widow of actor/director William Conrad (one of his many roles was in TV's *Jake and the Fatman* series). She had a number of her husband's items, such as scripts and photographs, that she wanted appraised and possibly sold. Valentino said, "As an afterthought she said, 'Oh, we've had this lead bird for the last thirty years sitting on a shelf in the TV room. Maybe you could take a look at it for me.' " Valentino knew that Conrad had been a director at one time at Warner's in the early 1960s. "I thought, this could be another Maltese Falcon but the odds are one in one hundred million," she said.

She went to the shipping department when the package

arrived and watched expectantly as the bird was pulled from the box and paper and bubble wrap were removed.

"When I looked at it, I saw that in fact it was the other Maltese Falcon," she said. "It had the correct prop number on the bottom and it had slash marks in the shoulder in front of the head and it was the perfect bronze color." The prop number was one later than the one on Milan's falcon.

Sachs explains that the scratch marks are on the breast because in the film Sydney Greenstreet, who plays the Fatman, scratches at the bird in a frenzy to peel the crust away to get to the gold and jewels underneath. Greenstreet finds that the Maltese Falcon is really made entirely of lead.

Why did Jack Warner give it to Conrad? That remains a mystery.

When the auction was announced, there was a great deal of interest and Valentino thought the bird might go for from $30,000 to $50,000, but soon realized the price would be higher. She called interested buyers and told them to prepare for six figures. The day of the auction the room was packed and the bidding soon reached $250,000. Then came a bid from a man in the back of the room who wore dark glasses, a hat, and a newspaper over his face. He bid $350,000, dropped the paddle that was used to show he wanted to bid, and walked out of the room. The newest mystery: Who was it? With commission the total price was $398,500, and the people at Christie's wondered if they would see the money.

They certainly did because the buyer was Ronald Winston, president of Harry Winston Jewelers, one of the most prestigious firms in the business.

Winston never allows himself to be photographed or interviewed in person and at the press conference to show off the bird, he sent a Humphrey Bogart look-alike. Winston was obviously the perfect person to own the bird and continue the mystery. During an interview he said, "I've always been a great fan of Bogart and love the movie because it deals with the intrigue and romance and search for something precious and that's what I do in my daily life is to try and find precious things . . . usually stones."

Soon after, Winston let it be known that he had sold his Maltese Falcon for a profit, but the exact price has never been revealed. Valentino said, "I heard it was sold for a million dollars to someone in Europe, but once more there's a mystery."

Then Winston set out to make his own version of the falcon. A mold of the original was clothed in four and one-half pounds of eighteen-carat gold and looked at the world with large Burmese ruby eyes. A forty-three-carat diamond hangs from a chain around its neck. Asking price is $8.5 million.

Winston said, "I wanted to bring the legend alive and finish the story that was never finished in the movie."

Milan feels all this makes his lead bird worth more, but he would not consider selling it. He has been offered considerably more than a million dollars recently, but turned it down. He says, "What would I do with the money? I'd probably go out and buy something else and I couldn't part with it. It's sort of part of me."

Milan has loaned his Maltese Falcon to the Warner Bros. Museum, which opened on the studio lot in 1996, so the elusive bird has now returned to its birthplace. It is on a perch on the wall above the Maltese Falcon exhibit and casts its aura of mystery over the room.

Milan says, "I come by and visit him and talk to him. He does talk, you know. He'd probably say, 'I am the stuff that dreams are made of.' "

Sachs adds, "All these props are the stuff and films are the stuff that dreams are made of. Dreams play an important part in our life."

Yes, it seems fitting that the search and everything surrounding the bird were shrouded in mystery. The moral in this seems to be, if you ever make a movie . . . keep the props!

CHAPTER 10

THE STEAMBOAT *ARABIA*

A chance meeting with a stranger led a family on an exhaustive search for a treasure ship under a Kansas farm.

Bob Hawley had been in the refrigeration and heating business in Independence, Missouri, for forty years when the saga began. His sons Greg and David worked with him, and the whole family loved the outdoors and shared a spirit of adventure. Greg and David had been drawn to the nearby mighty Missouri River since childhood. They had looked out at the murky water and imagined the things that had happened there.

They all enjoyed their work because it gave them the opportunity to be out with the public, calling on customers and checking on the heating and refrigeration work done by their company. One day in the mid-1980s David met a rather mysterious older man who was dressed entirely in black. The man told him he was looking for UFOs, Big Foot, and steamboats that had gone down in the Missouri River in the 1850s.

David knew he wasn't interested in UFOs or Big Foot, but the thought of sunken steamboats excited him. When he returned to the office, he told his father and brother about the eccentric fellow. The Hawleys were fascinated by the thought of finding one of those steamboats since they had all been interested in them and throughout their lives had heard stories about the legendary lost cargoes. When they stopped at their friend Jerry Mackey's local restaurant they told him the steamboat story and he, too, was intrigued by the idea.

David began to do thorough research and found that four hundred steamboats had been lost in the turbulent river in the mid-1800s. The golden age of steamboating was in the 1850s, when river traffic was at its peak. The muddy Missouri, which reaches from St. Louis to Montana 3,000 miles away, was the longest river in North America until modern engineering shortened it by a few miles, making the Mississippi the longest.

Steamboats were crucial to the communities all along the river, and if not for them, settlers and goods would never have arrived in the West. Those boats linked even the smallest communities to the large cities of this country and the world. Among the hundreds of tons of cargo that were shipped were fancy silks from France, expensive china from England, and more mundane items such as farming tools, pots and pans, and clothing.

Through the years the Missouri's swift stream eroded banks and caused a gradual change of the river's course. David learned that some of the sunken steamboats were now under farmland. By now the Hawleys and Jerry Mackey had a serious case of treasure fever. They would find one of those boats and salvage it. It didn't matter that it might be far under the ground and the task almost impossible. As Dave said, "No one else had ever done it so we would."

After three years of researching the location of ten steamboats, all under farmland, David was drawn to the last one on his list, which was described as the Great White Steamboat *Arabia.* Not only was there something captivating about the legend surrounding the sinking, the tons of varied cargo, and failed efforts at salvaging the boat, but it was under a farm in Kansas that was only a thirty-minute drive from their homes in Independence. The other steamboat sites were hours away. They all knew there was a tremendous amount of work ahead, and extra hours of driving to a site would have made things even more difficult. The *Arabia* site proved to be a lucky choice.

Although the Missouri River was a major commercial highway, it was a difficult and hazardous trip for the steamboats, especially going upriver from St. Louis. There was great danger of having the hull suddenly pierced by trunks of fallen trees, referred to as "snags," hidden from view, lurking just beneath the water. Since thirty cords of wood were burned each day to keep a steamboat running, many trees along the banks were cut, resulting in a tremendous number of snags.

David says, "A steamboat trip from St. Louis to Kansas City was more dangerous than today going to the moon."

Most of the steamboats had a life of about five years because of the difficult trips. The *Arabia* was built in 1853 and was three years old when she left St. Louis in late August

1856, for Sioux City, Iowa, and stops in between. About a week later, on the evening of September 5, a short distance above Kansas City, the great *Arabia* was torpedoed by a snag and began sinking immediately. Fortunately, all the people aboard, including many women and children, were saved, but 200 tons of cargo and a mule went to the bottom of the river. In addition to nearly everything that would have been for sale in 1856, the boat was said to also be supposedly carrying four hundred barrels containing premium-grade Kentucky bourbon whiskey. The loss of that whiskey promoted years of fruitless searching by all sorts of people, adding to the legend and mystique of the *Arabia.*

By using old river maps, David determined the *Arabia* was under the Kansas farm of Norman Sortor, who was well aware of the steamboat since his father and grandfather, owners of the farm before him, had talked about it. In the 1890s some men had worked diligently to uncover the elusive *Arabia* for only one reason, to get at that whiskey. They failed. Sortor was willing to let the eager treasure hunters try to find the boat, and entered into an agreement with them, but he couldn't help saying it would be an impossible task.

This in no way dampened anyone's enthusiasm, and in July 1987, David began walking through Sortor's field with a proton magnetometer, a device that locates iron, until he heard a signal and knew he had found the spot over the *Arabia.* Then he tied a surveyor's ribbon at the top of a tall cornstalk. The wreck was one-half mile from the river's edge and 45 feet underground.

Sixteen months later, the men and machines returned to begin raising the *Arabia.* There were now five partners, the three Hawleys and Jerry Mackey, as well as new member

David Luttrell, who joined the group after reading about the project in a newspaper article. He was in the construction business and had heavy equipment expertise. Removing the flood of water from the old underground river channel was a challenge twenty-four hours a day. They dug twenty wells, 65 feet deep, and water was pumped back into the river by a system designed by Bob Hawley. Four generators and twenty pumps were used. Mud engulfed them every day, but they were determined. Family and friends pitched in, and optimism was high even when they were nearly frozen.

Flo Hawley, Bob's wife and mother of Greg and David, kept a journal. Her entry for November 16, 1988: "Wet and tired. Temperatures below zero. Water table low enough only in winter to work. Knee deep in mud." She said, "I was worried from day one someone would be electrocuted. All that water and equipment."

Then a wonderful happening on November 28, 1988. They found the huge paddle wheel, 28 feet in diameter. It was the first find. The second cause for excitement was a small shoe caught in the spokes of the wheel. On the bottom was a mark indicating it was a Goodyear rubber shoe. The searchers agreed that it was like a gold bar in their hands. David says, "We all knew why we were there."

As the water went down they were able to glimpse the *Arabia*'s secrets, but then it would reflood. They had been working for two months and there had been only hints of what they might find. The partners got together and agreed they needed a bank loan of at least $50,000 to continue, but if their efforts failed, they would end up losing their homes. Should they cut their losses and stop? They decided to continue and took out the loan, the first of many.

The best day came in December when the first barrel appeared. When it was opened, there were Wedgwood china dishes and, altogether, 178 beautiful artifacts including silks from China, figurines and perfume bottles from France, and silverware. Bob called Flo at home and told her to get to the site right away. She told him she couldn't leave because she had chili cooking on the stove for dinner. Then, hearing his tone, she rushed down to the scene. She later said that finding the dishes was the turning point. They had thought they would sell whatever treasure items they might find, but realized they couldn't break up any part of *Arabia*'s cargo.

When they finished bringing up everything, there were 200,000 items that would take twenty years of cataloging. David said, "It was like an 1856 Wal-Mart." The treasure turned out to be the single greatest collection of pre–Civil War artifacts in the world. Besides the more specialized items like perfume and liquor, there were foods in jars and cans. Daring Jerry Mackey ate one of the 133-year-old pickles and said, "They are still fresh and sweet."

After the four-month recovery that completed the excavation on February 11, 1989, the *Arabia* was allowed to sink back into the ground. The partners decided to open a museum, but first almost three years of preservation work was needed. In the beginning, some fragile items were stored in Jerry Mackey's restaurant refrigerator so they would not disintegrate.

The Treasure of the Arabia Museum opened in Kansas City, Missouri, on November 13, 1991, three years from the day the excavation began. There has not yet been an official appraisal, but anyone looking at the astounding number of artifacts would easily estimate they are worth millions of dol-

Items recovered from the steamboat **Arabia.**

lars. However, the look into the history of life along the Missouri is priceless.

The fees charged for admission to the museum will help those diligent treasure hunters pay off their loans.

As the partners gaze at those 200,000 items in their museum, David Hawley sums up their feelings: "Nothing is more adventurous or exciting than finding buried treasure."

CHAPTER 11

Washington Inaugural Page

He fought the British and became our country's first president and father figure, yet what might be George Washington's most important writing was found in England.

In these days when polls seem to influence politicians' speeches, think of Washington, who did not need to worry about precedent and wanted to set forth his true thoughts in his first inaugural address. He had a great deal to say and labored on it at Mount Vernon until he had sixty-four pages, or thirty-two leafs, written on both sides, which are half the size of modern pages. Washington proudly showed his work to James Madison, and it is thought by scholars that Madison told him it was too long and too revolutionary. His advice seems to have been to make it shorter and less incendiary.

On the day of the inauguration, April 30, 1789, Washington arrived in the nation's first capital, New York City, by a barge especially built for him. From the balcony of the Fed-

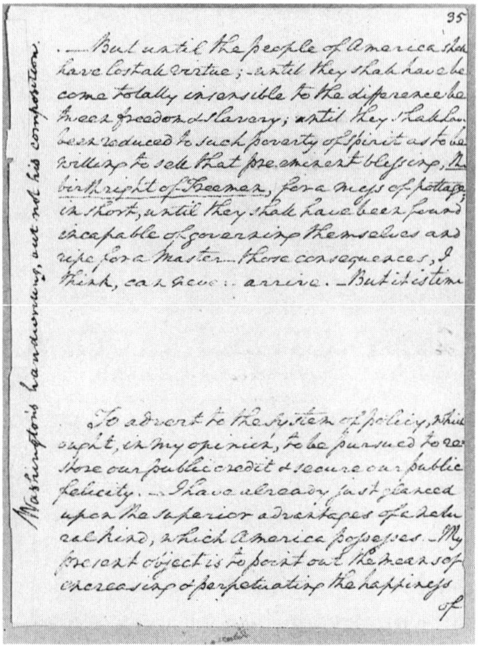

35

—But until the people of America shall have lost all virtue;—until they shall have become totally insensible to the difference between freedom & slavery;—until they shall have been reduced to such poverty of spirit as to be willing to sell that pre-eminent blessing, the birthright of Freemen, for a mess of pottage; in short, until they shall have been found incapable of governing themselves and ripe for a Master—those consequences, I think, can never arrive.—But it is time

To advert to the system of policy, which ought, in my opinion, to be pursued to restore our public credit & secure our public felicity.—I have already just glanced upon the superior advantages of the natural kind, which America possesses.—My present object is to point out the means of increasing & perpetuating the happiness of

Washington's handwriting, but not his composition.

A page from George Washington's original inaugural address.

eral Courthouse he delivered an eleven-page speech that was cautious and neutral. However, he did make reference to "the sacred fire of liberty . . . staked on the experiment entrusted to the hands of the American people." The other speech was packed away somewhere and possibly forgotten.

In 1996, Simon Roberts, a book specialist at Phillips auction house in London, went to a lovely country home in Suffolk, England, to make an appraisal of books, furniture, and other artworks prior to an estate sale. When Roberts had finished in the library, the gardener who was showing him around took him to another room and pointed out an object protruding from under the sofa, which turned out to be a pouch. Inside were a group of items including a large album. When Roberts removed it from its worn silk covering and opened it, he saw on the first page a manuscript in what he recognized as the handwriting of George Washington. There was also a report signed by Benjamin Franklin and a letter to Washington from the Marquis de Lafayette, the Frenchman who had come to help fight the Revolution and whom Washington thought of as the son he never had.

Roberts rushed the valuable documents back to Phillips so that the manuscript consultant, Felix Pryor, could evaluate them. When Pryor saw the Washington leaf, he said, "I knew it must be from the inaugural because I had heard about it and other leafs had been found. Washington had a very distinct handwriting."

Pryor also saw some writing on the edge of the page, which said, "Washington's handwriting but not composition." Pryor recognized this as the writing of Jared Sparks, a noted nineteenth-century biographer of Washington who later became president of Harvard.

Sparks had received Washington's papers from his heirs and, according to Pryor, didn't think Washington had written the long inaugural address but had just copied, in his own hand, notes by a speechwriter. So Sparks gave the pages away. In fact, he cut up some of the leafs so he would have more to give to anyone who seemed interested.

The specialists at Phillips, one of London's most respected auction houses, were convinced that the long inaugural address was definitely composed by Washington and the leaf they had, numbered 35 on one side and 36 on the other, was only the fourteenth ever to have been found and most likely the heart of the speech because of what it said.

Pryor said, "What we find in leaf 14 seems to represent something of an oratorical climax. Both its style and vision entitle it to consideration as the undelivered Gettysburg Address of the American Revolution."

Through the years the other thirteen pages had surfaced, having fortunately escaped Jared Sparks's scissors. There were markings on the Phillips leaf where Sparks had planned to wield his shears on that historic page, but fate had taken a hand and it was saved.

The saga of the saved leaf unfolds this way. A noted British geologist, Charles Lyell, on a visit to the United States in the 1840s met with Jared Sparks. When Lyell said his wife liked to collect documents, Sparks happily presented the Washington leaf to him for her collection. Luckily, Sparks gave whole pages to important people. The owners of the home where the page was found have steadfastly remained anonymous, but it is supposed that they are descendants of Charles Lyell. There has been no information on why the items were originally placed under the couch.

Charles Sachs, noted rare document expert says, "Back then people were as crazy as we are now to gather these things, but prices were very different. A glance at a catalog of the 1890s would show that Washington letters sold for $3 and a really good one for $15."

There was a great deal of excitement leading up to the Phillips auction of the Washington leaf on June 13, 1996. They valued it at between $150,000 and $200,000. In 1994 one of those thirteen other leafs had been sold at Christie's auction house in New York for $180,000.

The bidding began at £50,000, and in that electric atmosphere the price kept going up and up. Then came a bid on the phone for £180,000, which in U.S. money is $275,000, and the auctioneer's gavel signified sold. This set a world record for a Washington document. The buyer has continued to remain anonymous, which seems to be in keeping with the mystery of the lost speech, but Washington's message is now public and we can all share in the treasure.

He predicted the United States would be a world leader and would always preserve freedom. He also stressed education for everyone, which was considered radical at a time when only the rich were educated. Scholars feel that his words really called for the information highway of the future and were visionary.

Sachs says, "I think next to having your heroes over for dinner, having a document is as close as you can come to touching them and you certainly often touch their soul."

CHAPTER 12

THE HOXNE HOARD

When gray-haired Eric Lawes began searching with a metal detector for a friend's lost hammer in a farmer's field at Hoxne, Suffolk, England, November 16, 1992, he wasn't thinking of Julius Caesar and the Roman Empire, but he soon would.

Lawes had a signal from the metal detector and stooped down to brush the soil away at that spot. He didn't find the hammer but had come upon what appeared to be an ancient pure silver coin about the size of his thumbnail. He dug deeper and found more coins, not only silver but gold, and then silver spoons and gold bracelets. He knew that hoards of Roman coins had been found in England and realized the importance of his find. Lawes carefully placed the treasure in his car trunk and contacted the local authorities.

Britain had been an outpost of the Roman Empire. Julius Caesar arrived in 55 B.C., took a look around, fought some battles, and returned to Rome. Then in A.D. 43 Claudius subdued Britain and the Romans ruled for three and a half centuries. The rich farmland of what is now East Anglia, where Lawes found the coins, brought wealthy landowners who built palatial villas that long ago crumbled away.

Within a few hours Jude Plouviez, Suffolk's archaeology officer, joined Lawes at the scene. She said, "I think the 'oh my God' came when I saw the stuff in the back of Eric's car. It was the most amazing collection of Roman silver spoons, gold jewelry, and coins. I looked and I thought 'ah, it's real.' It really is a late Roman hoard and I was even more excited when I realized, talking to Eric, that it wasn't everything. There was even more in the ground. We could locate it and have a look at where it came from, which is really unusual. It was very exciting to have a look at the objects in proper context."

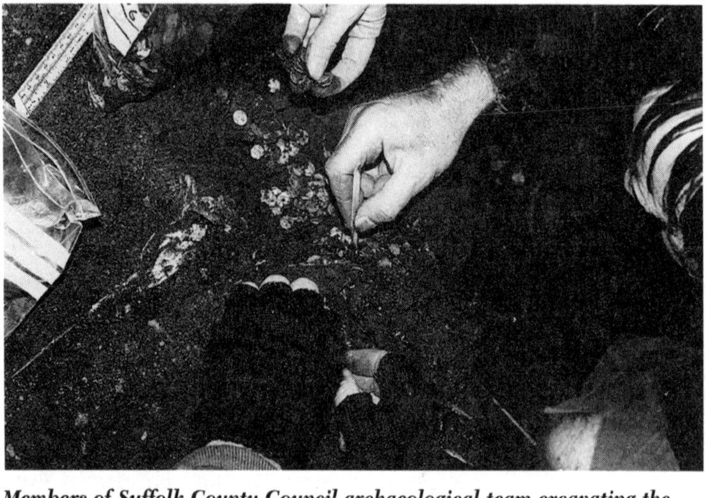

Members of Suffolk County Council archaeological team excavating the Hoxne treasure.

The next day Plouviez and a team from the county's archaeology unit laid a rectangle around the small hole of the original find and as they dug deeper they found more coins and objects in that tight area. She also found some metal hinges and surmised that the items were probably in a wooden box that had entirely decomposed. She said, "It was a quite shallow box, about 9 inches deep like a wooden drawer. The gold bracelets were extremely fine and very beautiful." They dug well into the night until they thought they had everything. The next morning the treasure was rushed to Curator of Antiquities Catherine Johns and her colleagues at the British Museum in London.

Johns was thrilled and amazed by the treasure and also by the fact that Plouviez had taken some of it out of the ground in large blocks of earth so they could determine just how it was packed. She said, "We knew it was a very large treasure with a huge amount of coins but we couldn't determine immediately the true extent or the date. It was enormously important, and still is, that most had been professionally excavated by Jude. Therefore, we had the proper archaeological records. Most people, when they find treasure, become very excited and carry on and take everything out of the ground. Mr. Lawes is a very calm, rational individual and he didn't do that. He contacted the proper authorities."

After the coins and other items were taken to the lab, they were all astounded at the size of the treasure. Plouviez had guessed there were about 5,000 coins, but in fact there were 14,875; 569 of them gold, 24 bronze, and the rest silver. The largest previous find of coins was 3,000, so Mr. Lawes had really hit the jackpot.

Plouviez said, "They were of high value. Not the kind of

things people would be carrying around as small change, but the sort of thing used to buy houses and land and pay taxes."

There was more than just coins to thrill everyone. There was the jewelry and complete sets of silver spoons. In fact, there were two hundred items in all.

Johns said, "Before Hoxne, the total find of silver spoons was eighty and from Hoxne there were seventy-eight, which nearly doubled the amount."

Plouviez said, "I've been an archaeologist for twenty-five years and it's the most dramatic thing I've ever found. A wonderful array of objects."

"The Roman gold in the jewelry is high purity," Johns said. "More than we have now. My favorite item is the handle from a silver vase that looks like a woman. Actually, she's a little silver pepper pot."

At the museum they also determined by the dates that the coins and other treasures were not buried before A.D. 407. Plouviez said it appeared that the people were in a hurry to leave. "There was lots of upheaval then in the Roman Empire. People were invading from the east."

Dr. Tom Plunkett, Keeper of Archaeology at the Ipswich Museum near Hoxne, who was also involved with the treasure, said, "It wasn't good to take large amounts of precious metal because you could be murdered for it along the way."

How like today! It seems that not much has changed in 1,600 years.

Plunkett also points out, "Just think how the treasure had been stacked in this little box and lain just under the ground for 1,600 years. All through the passage of history and all the great things that have happened in this country since: The Anglo-Saxons and the fighting, the Norman Conquest and the monasteries and Cardinal Wolsey and Henry the Eighth and goodness knows what. And that little box sat for 1,600 years about two feet under the ground just waiting for someone to find it."

Once the full extent of the treasure was known, the next question that had to be answered was: Whom would it belong to? In England there is a "Treasure Trove law." Treasure Trove may be defined as objects of gold or silver that have been deliberately hidden with the intention of recovery and of which the original owner cannot be traced. Any find that appears to qualify should be reported to the police and is subject to a coroner's inquest. If the jury at the inquest decides that the find satisfies these conditions, it is declared Treasure Trove and is the property of the Crown. It is then possible for the British Museum or another museum to acquire it on payment of a sum equal to its full market value as determined by an independent committee. That sum is passed on to the finder of the treasure by the Department of National Heritage as an *ex gratia* reward. Simply put: "Treasure Trove law says that it belongs to the state and the finder is rewarded with the market value." This certainly seems fair and should keep people out there looking!

The entire country waited with baited breath for the results of the coroner's inquest, to see what value the committee would place on one of the largest Roman treasures ever found in Britain.

The decision was one and three-quarter million pounds sterling, or in U.S. dollars just about three million. When the elderly Lawes was interviewed on television and asked what he would do to celebrate, he replied, "I haven't decided yet on a celebration." Then a reporter asked, "Don't you wish you were a little younger?" Lawes, in his understated way responded, "I certainly do."

Johns and Plouviez think that large silver platters and dishes, which would have been owned by the people who buried the Hoxne Hoard, are probably buried in another location. Perhaps they and other treasures from the Roman days will also be found accidentally.

In any event, Eric Lawes proved that it paid to be an honest man. By contacting experts he gained a fortune and provided a glimpse into history.

CHAPTER 13

TAMERLANE

Though this tale involves the author of books and stories of suspense, horror, and mystery, it has a happy ending for a young fisherman from Massachusetts who found something more valuable on land than he ever did at sea.

Since he wants to remain anonymous we will call him Ben. It was late February 1988 when he stopped in at a roadside antique barn in southern New Hampshire. He had been collecting books on local history for a few years and enjoyed browsing through New England shops. He went to a bin of early-twentieth-century pamphlets on fertilizers and farming machines. Since these were of no interest to him, he was about to walk away when a little book, actually more of a pamphlet, caught his eye. It was called *Tamerlane and Other Poems* and had a price tag of $15. Instead of an author's name it just said "by a Bostonian." Ben recognized the title because he had recently read *Yankee Bookseller,* the reminiscences of Boston book dealer Charles Goodspeed, who included a chapter on *Tamerlane.* He thought he had an important book because of the value placed on it by Goodspeed, and quickly bought it. That same day Ben called Sotheby's Boston office and took the book there.

After *Tamerlane* was sent to New York the next day to positively confirm its authenticity, Ben heard the good news. David Redden, executive vice-president of Sotheby's, said, "We opened the package and opening a package here is exciting because you might really have a treasure and this was. It was a wonderful discovery. Edgar Allan Poe's *Tamerlane* is the Holy Grail of American book collecting. It's the first edition of his first book and the most valuable rare book in American literature. Only eleven known copies existed before this one and most are in libraries or private institutions. Each copy since the 1950s sold for over $100,000."

Redden noted that Poe's work is the most valuable of that of any American writer. He wrote the first detective story, "The Murders In the Rue Morgue," and he was a master of suspense and an expert on Gothic romance and horror, but he never made much money in his short, tragic life. He died in Baltimore at forty under mysterious circumstances.

It certainly would have surprised Poe to know that the poems he wrote at ages thirteen and fourteen and that were published in 1827 when he was eighteen would become so valuable. At the time, the thin book sold for twelve and one-half cents, and no one knows how many copies were printed. The poems were full of adolescent angst and the forerunner of the romantic doom in his later work. A critic at that time said, "A book the critics read without praising, and the ladies praised without reading." It seems that the publisher

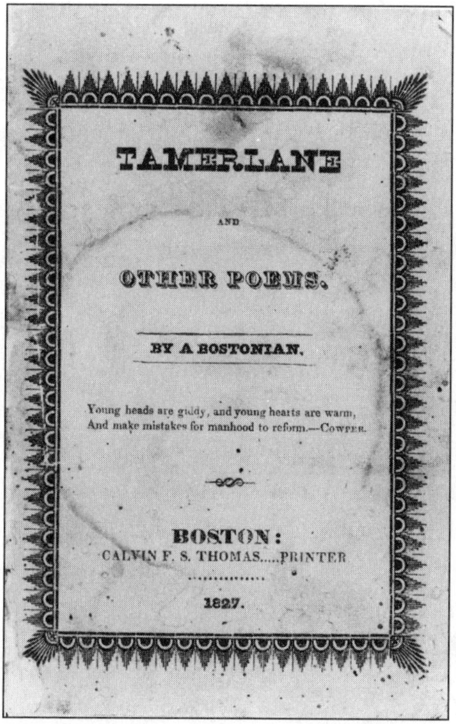

TAMERLANE

AND

OTHER POEMS.

BY A BOSTONIAN.

Young heads are giddy, and young hearts are warm,
And make mistakes for manhood to reform.—COWPER.

BOSTON:
CALVIN F. S. THOMAS.....PRINTER
....
1827.

Cover of *Tamerlane*, courtesy of the 19th Century Shop, Baltimore

***The cover of the first edition of Edgar Allan Poe's* Tamerlane.**

destroyed the unsold copies. However, when Poe wrote a preface to an 1829 reprinting of *Tamerlane* in Baltimore, he said that the 1827 version had been "suppressed through circumstances of a private nature." The rarity of the work and Poe's words have fascinated the book world ever since.

"The Raven" and "The Pit and the Pendulum" are probably Poe's most famous works, but according to Redden, they are not at the top of avid book collectors' wish list. It's *Tamerlane.*

"Poe emerged as one of the greatest writers of the nineteenth century," said Charles Sachs, noted manuscript expert. "He died young and there was not much product. He's avidly collected and the work is very scarce and that's a dangerous combination. It drives the price up."

The first copy of *Tamerlane* was not found until 1859 and was quickly bought by the British Museum. The second turned up in 1874, and when it was sold at auction in 1892 it brought $1,850, about the same price an Audubon folio, *The Birds of America,* was bringing at the time. By 1925 only four copies of Poe's book had been found. That year *The Saturday Evening Post* ran an article entitled "Have You a Tamerlane in Your Attic?" A Worcester, Massachusetts, woman who was living in an attic read the article. She had a *Tamerlane* that had been in her family for two generations. She contacted Boston dealer Charles Goodspeed, who sold it privately for $17,500, at the time the highest price paid for any American first edition.

It was Goodspeed's description of this sale and another he made because of the magazine article that formed the chapter in his book, the one Ben had read and the reason he bought his *Tamerlane.*

The eleventh copy, discovered in 1954, was sold at Sotheby's in 1974 for $123,000, again a record price for an American first edition.

On June 7, 1988, Ben's *Tamerlane* was sold at Sotheby's auction for $198,000. Redden said, "The fisherman is a shy man and brought his mother with him to the auction. After the shock wore off and we asked him what he would do with the money he said he would buy a new boat."

The new owner of *Tamerlane,* Richard Manney, was also

thrilled. He said that he had been a great reader as a child and when he was finally in a position to do so, he wanted to put together a collection of books that affected him then. Poe was an integral part of what he loved as a child.

"Poe was one of the great great writers of American literature," Manney said. "To be able to have a copy of his first endeavor, with only a handful in the world, was a great opportunity and I didn't want to let it go by. This is what the author held in his hands. This is how the publisher and printer decided this book should look. To have that original piece of work—it's something that's extraordinary!"

Redden said that treasures can often be lost. "*Tamerlane* could easily have been chucked out if not sold. Something that's worth $15 could easily be discarded. Something that's worth $200,000 gets looked after very very well and will be looked after forever very very well."

Which is more than what happened to poor Edgar Allan Poe.

CHAPTER 14

THE COLE YOUNGER GUN

The most valuable outlaw weapon of all time ended up in a safe deposit box belonging to a magician in southern California.

Early in 1997, Greg Martin, internationally known rare gun expert, collector, and consultant at Butterfield & Butterfield auctioneers in San Francisco, California, received a letter from a man who claimed to have the revolver taken from outlaw Cole Younger by the sheriff after the infamous Northfield, Minnesota, First National Bank robbery. The man wanted it appraised for possible sale.

Martin was always suspicious because he had seen many fakes through the years, so he was careful to check on the history of the weapon. He said, "It was a Smith and Wesson Model 3 Russian First Model Single Action Revolver and after I saw it I knew it would be worth at least $7,500 if it had no connection with the robbery, but if it did, it would be very valuable."

Cole Younger was such an important member of the notorious Jesse James gang that it was usually referred to as the James–Younger gang. They were always well armed, and their brazen and brutal bank and train robberies in the 1870s terrorized many people but left others admiring them as heroes. Their exploits were the basis of many books and Hollywood films, including the 1941 film *Bad Men of Missouri,* which starred Dennis Morgan and Jane Wyman. It was about Cole Younger and his gang. A 1972 film telling of their story, *The Great Northfield Minnesota Raid,* starred Robert Duvall and Cliff Robertson.

In March 1876, Jesse decided to bury millions of dollars the gang had stolen in the Wichita Mountains of Oklahoma. Other members of the gang were to share the treasure later on, and they all, including Cole Younger, wrote their names on a bucket that would be used as a clue to finding the money. Then the James–Younger gang turned their attention to what they considered "the big one," the robbery of the Northfield, Minnesota, First National Bank.

On September 7, 1876, about two P.M., the gang rode into Northfield to rob the bank. According to Martin, they had become a little careless in their methods, were poorly disguised, and failed to achieve the element of surprise. Jesse and Frank went into the bank while the other six, including Cole Younger and his two brothers, remained as lookouts outside. Unfortunately for the gang, the men in town had heard rumors about their plan and a bloody shoot-out followed. It was the first time the gang had encountered any opposition. When it was all over, two of the robbers were dead, as well as a bank cashier who was shot by Jesse James. Bob and Jim Younger, Cole's brothers, were wounded, as were many others. The remnants of the gang managed to make their getaway, closely pursued by the posse led by Sheriff James Glispin. Somewhere west of Mankato, Minnesota, Frank and Jesse James split off on their own, but Cole Younger stayed with his wounded brothers. It took two weeks for Sheriff Glispin and the posse to catch up with the Younger brothers in a river bottom thicket at Madelia, Minnesota. After a firefight, the gang surrendered to the posse and the Smith & Wesson revolver was taken from Cole Younger by Sheriff Glispin on September 21, 1876. Younger was quoted as having said to Glispin when he was captured: "Sheriff, I had the sure bead on you but you were too quick for me. It's all right."

Sheriff Glispin kept the gun because of the notoriety surrounding the crime. The story of the capture was so newsworthy that Mrs. Glispin compiled a scrapbook of articles surrounding the event and her husband's role in it. When the sheriff died, his wife eventually passed the gun and scrapbook on to her heirs. The items stayed in the family until they finally became the possession of Phillip Stocker, a descendant of Mrs. Glispin and the man who wrote to Greg Martin at Butterfield's.

Stocker, in his late fifties, was at one time in the computer programming business but changed careers and became a magician, something he had always wanted to do. Stocker said, "My father gave the gun to me when I was born. Actually it was left in a safety deposit box in a bank." About 1990 Stocker told his three children he would give each of them a piece of the gun every year. He was referring to the fact that a person can give someone up to $10,000 per year tax free and thus avoid inheritance taxes after he or she has passed

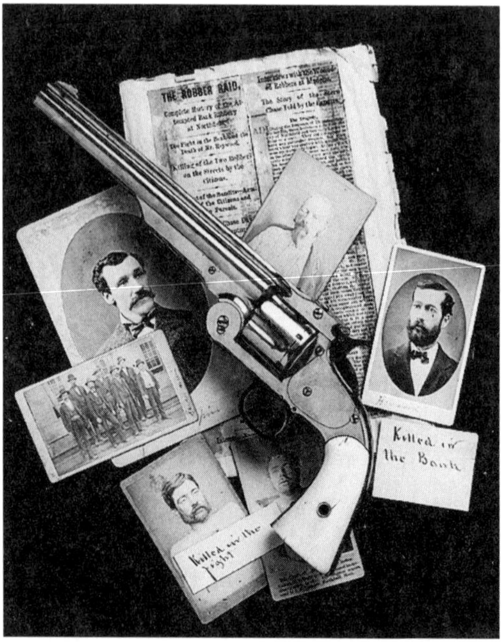

Cole Younger's gun and pieces from the scrapbook devoted to the outlaw.

away. In 1997 Stocker decided to take the gun out of the safe deposit box where it had rested for more than eighty years and have it appraised by an expert.

Once Martin received all the other materials from Mrs. Glispin's scrapbook and signed notes by Sheriff Glispin, he was impressed by the impeccable history of the gun and was convinced it was the real thing. Stocker decided to have the Smith & Wesson revolver sold at auction at Butterfield & Butterfield in San Francisco in August 1997. The scrapbook and related materials would be included in the sale. In the catalog the price was estimated at $50,000 to $60,000. It turned out to be a low figure, for the gun was sold for $211,000. Martin said, "This is the highest price ever paid for an outlaw gun and makes Cole Younger's gun the most valuable outlaw weapon of all time." The delighted Stocker said that the money will put his three children through school and much more.

The buyer, who prefers to remain anonymous, is a businessman and gun collector and friend of Martin's. After the sale Martin thought it would be interesting to fire the gun for the first time since Cole Younger had done so. The new owner gave his permission, but before Martin could do this, he needed to find special black powder bullets, as regular bullets can't be used in a gun that is more than one hundred years old. The proper bullets were finally located, and Martin went to a secluded area and fired that famous and valuable outlaw weapon. He definitely enjoyed the experience.

And what happened to the gang that buried the treasure? Jesse James was killed April 13, 1882, and his brother Frank later stood trial and was acquitted of past crimes. About 1903 Frank turned up in Oklahoma searching for the buried money, but before he arrived, Cole Younger, who had served twenty-five years in prison, was already there looking for his share of the wealth. Other former gang members who had put their names on the bucket also tried their luck. None of them ever found the treasure. Ironically, it was Phillip Stocker, the owner of Cole Younger's gun, who really reaped the rewards, which just goes to show that fate seems to be fickle—or perhaps careful when it comes to bestowing treasure!

CHAPTER 15

The Roosevelt Ring

Our thirty-second president, Franklin Delano Roosevelt, was the only U.S. president to be elected for four terms. After the Japanese bombing of U.S. Navy ships at Pearl Harbor, Honolulu, Hawaii, many lives were lost. Roosevelt's words declaring America's entry into World War II, "December 7, 1941—a date which will live in infamy," are some of the most remembered in United States history. More than half a century later, Hawaii became important to the Roosevelt family once again when a treasured keepsake was lost there, seemingly forever.

There was a tradition in the Roosevelt family that the eldest son would give the family ring to his eldest son and so on down the line.

President Roosevelt's family had quite a lineage. His mother's family, the Delanos, claimed they could trace their roots back to the eleventh century and were descendants of

William the Conqueror. Between the Delanos and the Roosevelts, they claimed twelve ancestors who arrived on the *Mayflower.*

The Roosevelts came from Holland, where the name means "field of roses"—and that was their business, growing roses. Appropriately there are raised roses on the family crest. In the late 1600s the first two Roosevelt brothers to arrive in this country settled in Manhattan, New York. The firstborn brother was wearing the ring. After the death of President Roosevelt, April 12, 1945, his eldest son, James, received the gold-and-bloodstone ring with the family crest.

James Roosevelt followed his father's footsteps into politics and was a U.S. congressman from California for six terms. Since he married more than once, he had two fami-

Franklin Roosevelt wearing his family ring on his left hand.

lies with firstborn sons and faced a dilemma when it came to his father's ring. He gave it to his eldest son from his first marriage when he was grown. Then, while the eldest son, Del, from his second family was growing up, James decided to have another ring made with the family crest so he could give it to him. He wanted to avoid favoritism. James wore the ring himself until it was time to give it to Del Roosevelt so that it wouldn't be just another ring, but a true family heirloom. Once Del received the ring, he always wore it.

Red-haired, husky Del Roosevelt followed family tradition and is a Long Beach, California, city councilman. He's been told he looks like his grandfather's distant cousin, red-haired Teddy Roosevelt, avid outdoorsman, leader of the legendary Rough Riders in Cuba during the Spanish-American War, and twenty-sixth president of the United States.

Teddy Roosevelt is actually Del's great-great-uncle, and Del says he is the only family member besides Teddy to have red hair. He adds a bit of family history: "Teddy Roosevelt was my grandmother Eleanor's uncle and he raised her. He also introduced her to Franklin."

Along with the red hair, Del appears to have also inherited Teddy Roosevelt's love of the outdoors and the sea. During a Thanksgiving holiday in Hawaii with his wife, Jan, in 1990 they visited friends on Kauai at Hanalei Bay.

Because Del loves body-surfing, the couple went to the other side of the island to Brenneckey's Beach, a well-known site for that sport. It had been raining the first days of their vacation, but now the sunshine brightened their spirits and it seemed a perfect day for the sea.

Del says, "Twenty yards off the beach there was a sand bar and a channel to walk through. The water was about four and a half feet deep and came up to my waist but reached to Jan's shoulders. As she tried to walk to the island she lost her footing and began floating away but was soon able to get back to the beach." What Del didn't know at the time was that in that area, the 6- to 9-knot current known as the "freight train" could rob visitors of their rings and jewelry in a flash.

He continues: "As Jan reached out and I grabbed her hand, her hand slipped away and pulled the ring off my finger and down it went. I could see the glitter as it was going down into the silt." When he saw that Jan was okay, Del frantically tried diving for it, without success. He went to a youngster nearby and borrowed his face mask and continued the search for another half hour. Suddenly, Del saw a man nearby floating underwater with a metal detector.

It was Dutch Medford, legendary treasure hunter, who with his wife had found and returned to owners nearly $400,000 worth of rings, jewelry, and assorted valuables lost on the beaches. One of his more amazing discoveries was the high school ring of a Hawaiian resident who had lost it thirty-seven years before. Medford saw the initials in the ring and contacted the high school. When he found the name of the owner, he was able to find the man, who, naturally, was ecstatic.

Medford found his first treasure at eight when he discovered a Mason jar filled with silver coins on the family ranch in Texas. He was hooked and became a treasure hunter from that day on. In 1988 he and his wife moved to Hawaii where he became a dealer for White Metal Detectors. This allowed him to spend part of every day on the beaches and in the ocean with his metal detector. Whenever he found something, he made every effort to locate the owner by using any clues he could find. His detective work paid off, to the delight of people who thought they would never see their precious items again.

Of course, there were times he couldn't find the owner but nevertheless kept the rings or other jewelry, hoping that at some time he would find them.

Naturally, Roosevelt didn't know of Medford's successes at the time. He was just hoping the metal detector would help and asked Medford if he had ever found any rings. When the answer was yes, Del asked him to look for his lost ring. Medford tried for an hour but was forced to give up because the current made the search exhausting.

The Roosevelts had to leave the next day. Dejectedly, Del gave Medford his name and phone number just in case he found the ring. He explained how important it was to him, especially because his father was ill and would be terribly upset if he knew the ring was missing.

Before the Roosevelts left Hawaii, they happened to talk with a shaman, who assured them it was predestined that the ring would be found because it had been in cleansing water. They hoped his words would one day prove to be true, but had to return home empty-handed and disappointed, believing they would never see the ring again.

Medford began to search for the ring two days a week for about four hours each day until April 1, when the tides changed. He said, "The six-foot waves wiped out much sand and exposed rocks. I went into the water and found a large rock we call the grinding stone and I searched around the rock with the metal detector. I had a signal and then it became stronger and there it was. A wide gold band sticking out of the water. I was so excited I jumped up out of the water and shouted 'alright' and eight other people reached for the ring, but I held tight."

Medford rushed home with the ring and showed it to his wife. Then he made a call to Roosevelt. He asked him, "Do you have three roses at the top of your ring?" Roosevelt was thrilled. He later said, "If it were me I'd probably keep it. You know that old saying about finders keepers, but Dutch tries to return everything. And he never takes anything for it. It's unbelievable. It's amazing. I felt like getting on a plane and going over there to give him a big hug and kiss."

Roosevelt told his father, James, how the ring had been found. "He was delighted," Roosevelt said. "It was so important that I could show it to my father because he died soon after. Now I will be able to give it to my eldest son James when the time comes and I'll probably make one for my other son Hall."

The shaman was right, and perhaps the spirits brought Medford to the water at the proper time. He says, "That's the real fun of treasure hunting, being able to return things to people who really believe they will never see them again, especially those things lost in the ocean. The look on people's faces is just absolutely priceless."

The Roosevelts and their sons spent Thanksgiving 1998 with the Medfords and plan to return each year at this time to be with their dear friends. This treasure of friendship means so much to them.

CHAPTER 16

THE QUEEN OF TREASURE HUNTERS

When the doctor delivered the words *You must retire,* they were like a death sentence to the slim, vibrant woman, who put up a brave front but was barely able to hold back the tears.

Kay Modgling was a surgical nurse twenty-five years ago and loved her work. In her mid-fifties, she couldn't believe that her recent health problems were more than overwork and the lingering aftereffects of the flu. When the diagnosis was congestive heart failure, she told herself she could overcome this with willpower and some rest. But these had not been enough, and the doctor was determined to convince her that in order to live, she had to change her life.

"What will I do if I'm retired?" she asked. "I need to keep busy. Have purpose to my life."

"The first thing you must do is walk, walk, walk," the doctor responded.

"But that's so boring," Kay replied.

"If you want to live, you'll walk," the doctor said sternly.

Days passed and Kay tried to be hopeful as she began walking around her neighborhood, but the more she saw older people slowly trudging along she imagined herself as one of them, and for the first time in her life she knew how depression felt. One day her sister-in-law came to visit on her way to an outing at the beach. She had a metal detector with her and showed Kay how it worked. When she saw Kay's dejected expression, she put the detector into Kay's hand and said, "Take this and start going out to the beach. It's amazing what you can find and the ocean air will do wonders for you."

The first day Kay went to Huntington Beach, California, with her metal detector, she found a number of coins. Just hearing the *beep-beep* sound that the detector made gave her a feeling of excitement. As she scooped up the sand at the indicated spot, she knew she had found something to keep her active and interested.

Kay's husband, Tom, began to hunt with her and they learned quickly and well. She said, "I've been on the beach after a storm and at times have found as many as 1,300 coins. I had to walk back to my car stooped over because of all those coins in my apron."

Soon Kay took her trusty detector to other areas, such as parks and campgrounds. Before long she not only had thousands of coins but quite an array of rings, watches, military medals, religious medallions, foreign currency, and gold and silver jewelry. She wished she could return all the items to their owners—after all, she had the keepsakes of a thousand courtships, marriages, and school graduations. Alas, there

Kay Modgling, surrounded by a portion of her finds.

rarely was any way to trace the treasures to their owners. Whenever she saw initials in a class ring that identified the school, she called the school (if she could find where it was) and asked for help in finding the owner. Unfortunately, many times the people at the schools did not want to take the time to help.

However, Kay was able to return one school ring because of her picture on the cover of a treasure magazine. In the picture Kay was surrounded by some of the thousands of items she had found, including school rings. Fourteen years later, a man who was working in his garage found a pile of old magazines, one of them, *Western and Eastern Treasures,* with Kay's picture. As he looked at it he recognized the ring Kay was holding as the high school graduation ring he had lost years before. He rushed to the phone and called the magazine. Soon he was able to meet with Kay, and she gave him the ring. They both cried because it meant so much to them.

Kay's fame reached law enforcement officials. Near her home in southern California, local police department detectives had searched for two and a half days for a gun that had been used as a murder weapon. Then they came to Kay for help. They took her to the most likely area and, with her detector, in fifteen minutes she found the gun in some ivy. "That really scared me," she said. "That barrel was pointing right at me."

At one point Kay used some of the coins she had found to buy a new Ford Pinto. Yes, there were that many thousands of dollars in coins, with many left over. About 1990 she stopped counting her finds because they numbered half a million and were valued at more than $60,000. She never sold anything and kept the valuable items in a safe deposit box at the bank. Kay was able to help some people who came to her because they had just lost rings or valuables in a particular area. She would go there with her detector and sometimes find the important keepsake. One day, when asked to find a diamond wedding ring lost on the beach, husband Tom came to the rescue. Kay's detector batteries were low and Tom quickly found the ring, which thrilled the previously despondent owner. So many rings are lost at the beach, Kay said. "When people are in the water their hands shrink and rings fall off. Rings should be put somewhere else when you're going into the water."

Kay and Tom would often go to parks before dawn to hunt. Some years ago in a park at four A.M. Tom found a little boy of five or six, asleep in the bushes. When the Modglings called the police, they were hesitant to come to the scene because they thought it might be some type of setup. Eventually, the police arrived and realized the treasure hunters had found a most important treasure. It turned out that the parents were drunk and had left the sleeping child alone in the park.

"I've been all over this country and others such as Mexico and Australia," Kay said. "All over the place and I've yet to go out and find nothing. I always find something." She described her trip to Australia as a fantastic experience. "I found a gold nugget that looks like a koala bear and it became a good luck charm."

Kay's prowess with the metal detector inspired many others who wanted to add some adventure to their lives or to find a way to overcome health problems and have fun while doing so. She said, "This hobby has given me my life. Whenever my health problems would bother me I'd just take my detector and away I'd go and just work off steam. I'm living proof that there's treasure everywhere, no matter where you find it."

In 1998, Kay passed away unexpectedly. She had overcome so many catastrophic illnesses, including several bouts with cancer, that her family and friends began to feel she could beat almost anything. She leaves a lasting legacy and was certainly a treasure to her family and all who knew her.

CHAPTER 17

Dinosaur Named Sue

Famous and accomplished people throughout history have had all sorts of places and things named for them, but who can claim a dinosaur with the same name? Sue Hendrickson can!

Peter Larson had only one ambition from the time he was four years old, and that was to be a dinosaur hunter. Luckily he was born and raised near one of the few places where fossils are found, the Bad Lands of western South Dakota. Almost all his waking hours were devoted to searching for the remains of those gigantic monsters who roamed the earth 65 million years ago. Even among dinosaurs there is the one most prized, the rarest and most valuable, the ultimate treasure—the *Tyrannosaurus rex,* the largest land predator known. It was Larson's lifelong dream to find one. As of 1990 there were only fifteen known specimens in the world, and none were more than half complete.

Larson founded the Black Hills Institute of Geological Research in Hill City, South Dakota, in 1968 when he was in his twenties. After his younger brother Neal graduated from college, he joined him at the Institute, which in terms of business is the largest of its kind in the United States selling fossils. Here, after the specimens are found, they are preserved and a mold is prepared for the life-size casts that are then made of the fossils. These are sold to museums all over the world so that people can view exact replicas of these prehistoric creatures. According to Larson, fossils can be found only where they lived and where their remains are preserved. The rocks must be the correct age and the erosion of the land such that the fossils finally come to the surface. They have been found in the United States as far south as New Mexico and up into Canada, in an area that cuts a swath through Colorado, Wyoming, the southwestern tip of South Dakota, and Montana.

"When searching for fossils you just have to walk and climb slowly with your eyes on the ground," Larson says. Even a tiny fragment is important and can easily be missed.

On an August day in 1990, Larson and a crew were working at a site when a member of the team and a friend of Larson's, Sue Hendrickson, wandered off on a lunchtime hike. Larson says that amateurs were often used to help in the hunt for fossils. He describes Hendrickson as an extraordinary amateur since she didn't have a degree in paleontology, but had a great deal of experience in and knowledge of fossils. After she had gone some distance, she stopped to examine the ground and recognized some fossil fragments. She stooped to get a better look and found a large object that resembled a fossil vertebra. She had an idea of what it was but needed confirmation from Larson, so she immediately returned to the site, treasure in hand.

He said, "When I saw it I knew it was the vertebra of a *T. rex* and I asked, 'Is there more?' and she said, 'Lots more.' I ran the two miles back to the site and when I saw what was there, I knew it was the best thing we would ever find. The best thing we would ever collect."

It was the first *T. rex* he had ever come across outside of a museum. The remains were under 50 feet of overburden, which Larson explains as sediment of dirt and rock accumulated through millions of years. They could see that there was nearly an entire skeleton of the *T. rex,* but it would be difficult and painstaking work to free it. In fact, they found that Sue was 90 percent intact and the largest *T. rex* ever found, measuring 41 feet from head to tail. The enormous skull was 5 feet in length.

Larson said that you just can't tie a piece of rope to the tail and pull it out. They had to remove the overburden because the *T. rex,* which was quickly named Sue in honor of its discoverer, was in a precarious position. The team, naturally including Hendrickson, had to begin 30 feet above Sue and work down. It was seventeen days of nonstop labor that required a variety of tools, including very tiny ones used to free the smallest fragments. The bones had to be encased in plaster casts, and fragments had to be glued together to fortify Sue for the 150-mile trip back to the Institute.

Once there, Larson and the others found that the left side of Sue's face was badly damaged and the left side of the lower jaw had been pulled out of the socket and pulled away, which had probably ended the *T. rex*'s life. Two smaller *T. rex* skulls were found nearby, leading Larson to suspect that per-

The head of the T. rex *discovered by Sue Hendrickson.*

haps it was a family left to die in the stream after a ferocious battle with another *T. rex.*

They also found a tooth fragment in Sue's rib, a gouge in her head, and evidence that the bone from a broken leg had healed. This led to speculation that possibly other *T. rex*'s had come to Sue's aid and nursed her back to health while her leg mended.

Sue had been found on a ranch in Faith, South Dakota, belonging to Maurice Williams, a Cheyenne River Sioux. While Larson and his team were digging out Sue's remains, he had immediately offered Williams $5,000 for Sue, and he accepted the offer. It was the first time anyone had paid for a fossil while it was still in the ground.

That was but a small amount of what it would cost to prepare Sue properly to be the featured exhibit at the Black Hills Institute. It would be the culmination of Larson's dream. Hendrickson had not only found a *T. rex* for Larson, but the biggest and best anywhere. Sue was the only *T. rex* 90 percent complete, and she was the largest at 41 feet from head to tail.

Larson estimated thirty thousand hours would be needed to prepare Sue and make the molds and casts. The cost would be at least $750,000. The work began and then trouble set in, which seemed to be in keeping with Sue's difficult life.

One morning in 1992, Larson, whose home was right behind the Institute, heard a knock at the door. An employee of the Institute shouted, "The place is crawling with FBI agents and the sheriff." Unbelieving, Larson rushed outside to see FBI agents, men from the sheriff's department, and the National Guard carrying boxes containing Sue out of the Institute and placing them on trucks.

"We're seizing Sue," Larson was told. They had a warrant for her arrest.

Maurice Williams had gone to a United States attorney and claimed rights to Sue. He had learned that Sue was quite valuable and worth much more than he was paid. The court determined he did own her because she was classified as real estate. Since the land Williams owned was on the Cheyenne River Sioux reservation, the federal government held it in trust. Government treaties differ from tribe to tribe, and in this case Williams could own his property. Until a disposition of Sue's remains could be made, she would remain in the custody of the federal government.

Larson, his brother, and other employees of the Institute were charged with 148 felony counts and 5 misdemeanors, including illegal trafficking in fossils and stealing them from tribal lands. Eventually they were all cleared except for Larson, who was convicted of two unrelated customs violations and was sent to federal prison for twenty-two months.

While Larson was in prison, executives of Sotheby's auction house in New York, who had heard about Sue, contacted Maurice Williams and the tribal council, offering to sell Sue at auction. The council and government said okay, and the sale was scheduled for October 4, 1997. It was the first time a dinosaur had ever been auctioned at Sotheby's. Larson was not able to attend because he had been released from prison but was still under house arrest, which meant he could not go farther than 50 feet from his home.

Sue Hendrickson was at the auction to bid farewell to her namesake, along with Terry Wentz from the Black Hills Institute, who had spent two thousand hours preparing Sue. It was an emotional time for them. Based upon her research, Hendrickson had new information on Sue, who had been referred to as female after she was named. Hendrickson said, "It seems to hold true that with the *T. rex* the robust, larger ones are female and the smaller ones are male." She laughed and added, "It shows that the biggest, worst carnivores in the world are women."

The room was packed and the auction began with David Redden, executive vice-president of Sotheby's, as auctioneer. Bids started at $500,000 and moved up quickly. Eight minutes later, Sue was sold for $7.6 million ($8.3 million with commission, which is 10 percent buyer's premium) to the Field Museum in Chicago, Illinois, the leading paleontological institute in the country. The funds to buy Sue had come from various sources in addition to the museum. The money from the sale was to be held in trust by the government for Maurice Williams.

The saga of Sue seems to be in keeping with the dangerous and difficult life she led, based upon her injuries. Even in death, 65 million years later, there continued intrigue, court battles, and displacement. Sue was not permitted to rest in peace in the Black Hills Institute, but was seized by the FBI and stored in the South Dakota School of Mines in Rapid City, South Dakota, by the federal government. Then she was transported in 130 crates to Sotheby's in New York and finally traveled to her new and permanent home in Chicago's Field Museum. This monster of all monsters was certainly not going to have an easy time of it, no matter what.

So just when all seemed lost for Peter Larson, fate sent him a gift. Stan Sacrison, an electrician by day and fossil hunter on the weekends, was out pursuing his hobby when he saw some fragments that he thought must be the real thing. He had heard about Larson, so came to him for expert advice. Amazingly, he learned that he had found the prize, a *T. rex*, smaller than Sue but 66 percent complete. It was a one in a million happening. Now Larson had a *T. rex* to proudly exhibit at the Institute and, appropriately, named the new star Stan. As of early 1999 there are now twenty-one *T. rex*'s in the world. The last six, including Sue and Stan, were found in the same general area.

Visitors to the Field Museum can see Sue being prepared in a special fossil lab, and in the year 2000 she will be ready to face the world in an exhibit of her own. Through the years, studies of Sue will provide information never before possible. Fortunately, millions of people will be able to see and marvel at the treasure that is Sue.

Hendrickson said, "The discovery and initial preparation of Sue were wonderful times. She is really incredible. There is so much to be learned from this one specimen. Even months and years later I can still hardly believe that I found her!"

What's next for the fascinating woman who is interested in so many things? She was diving in Egypt with the European Institute for Underwater Archaeology, mapping the submerged ancient royal port of Alexandria, which includes Antirrhodos Island, the site of Cleopatra's palace. She said she will also be diving in the Philippines. No matter what amazing treasure she finds next, it seems certain she will discover the unexpected.

CHAPTER 18

THE MOJAVE NUGGET

The gold rush never ended for Ty Paulson. More than a hundred years after James Marshall discovered gold in 1848 at Sutter's sawmill on the American River in northern California, Paulson relentlessly pursued his dream just as those forty-niners did.

He was so driven to find the elusive metal that he devoted his life to the search, giving little time to his family and living for years out of his old camper. He would spend his days wandering the deserts of California, certain his theories of where the gold should be would pay off.

The lure of treasure had always been with him. At first he tried diving in Cuba, then digging in Oklahoma, but then the gold fever hit and there was no cure. Family and friends who knew him said it wasn't financial reward that drove him but the need to be out in the wilderness and prove he could find gold.

Treasure expert and gold prospector Roy Roush was a friend of Paulson's and says, "Ty had theories about where the gold came from and this had to do with the continuous erosion of the earth's surface. He thought that ancient rivers, millions of years ago, had washed some of the gold loose from its place of origin in the mountains and deposited it in the dried-up riverbeds in the Mojave Desert of southern California. Through the years erosion of the soil brought the gold closer to the surface so that what couldn't be found in the 1800s could be found in this century. Ty was using an accepted theory, but adapting it to his hopes and dreams. He was very innovative and had something special. He could read the terrain."

Roush points out that the gold that we hear about as nuggets found in various parts of this country and the world is known as placer gold. This means it has come loose from the original vein. It was this placer gold that Paulson hoped to find.

Roush said that Paulson thought that since a mine detector could pick up metal and gold was a metal, he would use this device. This led to the discovery of larger nuggets. According to Roush, this led him to be the first person to use a metal detector to find gold and enabled him to find even more.

In the 1970s, Paulson contacted Wayne Leicht, noted gold and gem dealer in Laguna Beach, California, and sold him a one-pound nugget. Leicht says, "He had a nose for gold. He told me he had a three-pound nugget he would bring in and I also bought that one."

Any money Paulson made was used to buy necessary supplies so he could get back to the desert. He then devised a more effective method of searching the vast area. He could cover only so much ground walking with his metal detector in hand, so he attached a boom with a metal detector on the end of it to the front of his jeep. This way he could drive around, and when he had a signal from the detector, he would stop and use his handheld metal detector to pinpoint the exact location.

Ty Paulson's thirteen-pound gold nugget, dwarfing a dime used to indicate scale.

It was an autumn day in 1977 when Paulson heard a loud response from his detector. His daughter says that he told her it was a "zing," and not like the sound associated with anything he'd dug up before. He had to dig down about 18 inches and there it was, a thirteen-pound gold nugget. "Nothing would be like finding that nugget," she said. "He brought it over to show me and wasn't sure what he wanted to do with it."

According to his daughter, at first Paulson kept his treasure hidden in his camper, then he buried it for several months. Finally, it became a problem because he wasn't sure what he wanted to do with it or where it would be safe, and he decided to sell. He contacted Leicht.

"It was late at night when he brought it in. It was wrapped

in a yellow shirt," Leicht said. "He said, 'I've found it,' and then dropped it down on my desk and I heard a thud. One thing about Ty, he would never let anyone know where he found his gold. When I asked him the location of the nugget he said that if you draw a fifty-mile-radius circle around the town of Mojave you'd find it somewhere in there. Well, that's a very big area. We named it the Mojave Nugget because it was found in that desert." The nugget has also been referred to as the Mojave Queen.

Leicht has declined to give the sale price but says that the price of gold was high at the time and a nugget can be worth four or five times more than the price by weight.

Roush said, "It was the largest existing nugget ever found in California and maybe in the United States or even in North America. There were larger nuggets found during the gold rush days, but they were all melted down. Based on the weight it would be worth $75,000 but the size makes it more valuable. It could be worth up to $500,000 to a buyer who wants this one-of-a-kind nugget."

Paulson died several years after the culmination of his lifelong quest. His daughter feels he always knew he would find the big one, although that optimism was probably mixed with the thought that it might never happen. But it did. She said that her father felt he had proven his erosion theory of where the gold would be because the nugget was found in a dried-up riverbed.

Leicht sold the Mojave Nugget to a collector. He, in turn, loaned it to the Los Angeles Natural History Museum, where it has been displayed for several years.

There have been other amazing discoveries of gold, but probably none of the finders has devoted an entire lifetime to the search as Paulson did. In Victoria, Australia, in 1980, a couple and their children, using a metal detector found a sixty-one-pound, eleven-ounce nugget about 6 inches underground behind their mobile home. The following year this largest nugget in the world was sold to the Golden Nugget Hotel and Casino in Las Vegas, Nevada, for a million dollars. "The Hand of Faith," so named because it looks like a hand, has been on display there ever since. Many exceptionally large nuggets have been found in Australia, most of them in desolate areas.

Geologist George Wheeldon of Placerville, California, says that only about 10 percent of the gold in the world has been recovered—so for all of you who dream of treasure, take heart and go forth for gold!

CHAPTER 19

Crater of Diamonds State Park

There is only one place in the whole world where you can search for a diamond and keep what you find, regardless of value. You can't do it in South Africa or Australia, where the majority of the world's diamonds are found, but you can in Arkansas. In Crater of Diamonds State Park near Murfreesboro in the southwest corner of the state, more than seventy thousand diamonds have been found, some of them worth hundreds of thousands of dollars. For a small daily fee you can spend the day or days, weeks, and even years sifting through soil and rocks for that precious gem. It's not the pot of gold at the end of the rainbow—more like the precious rock in the bottom of the bucket.

It wasn't always this way. In August 1906 farmer John Wesley Huddleston's plow turned up a three-carat white stone, the first diamond found in America. Local historians say he was a man who hated farming his 160 acres and preferred the life of a prospector, so he often wandered the woods looking for gold. After news of his diamond spread, Huddleston accepted the offer to sell his property for $36,000, hoping to live in luxury for the rest of his life.

He spent the money as though there were no tomorrow. He even promised suitors that there would be a $1,000 dowry for each of his five daughters, but the money ran out before the first daughter was married. In his later years, when he could no longer work, the people of the community helped feed him.

Various mining companies began working the site after Huddleston's sale until the 1940s, without much success. Some valuable diamonds were found, but the companies were beset by all sorts of problems, including legal complications. In the 1950s, a firm bought the park and turned it into a private tourist attraction. People could hunt for diamonds, under the condition that if one was found, they had to split the price with the property owners if it was sold. In 1969 the property was sold to a Texas corporation, and in 1972 the state of Arkansas purchased the land after which the property became a 72-acre state park whose "diamond mine is a 36-acre 'field of dreams.' " Throughout the eroded surface of an ancient gem-bearing volcanic pipe, more than 21,000 diamonds have been found since 1972.

More than six hundred diamonds are found each year, and since 1972, 628 diamonds over one carat have been found. Park Superintendent Michael Hall says that 80 percent are industrial grade and 20 percent are gem quality. Very few places in the world have diamonds, and Arkansas ranks up there with Australia and Africa as having produced a large number of quality gems. Most diamonds at the park

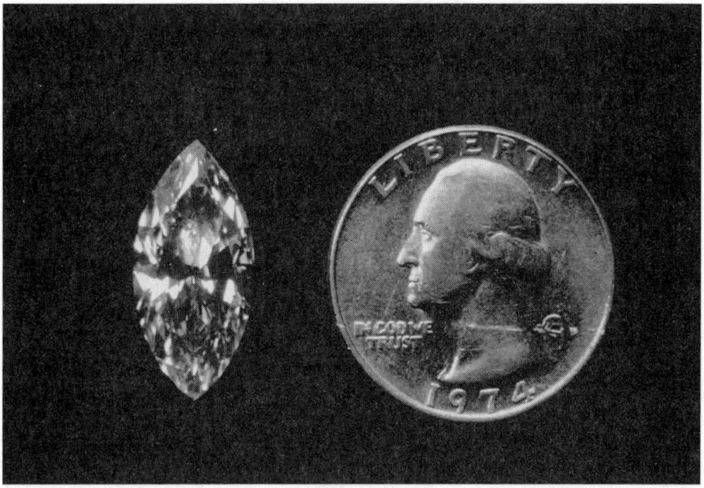

The Amarillo Starlight, the largest diamond ever found by a visitor since Crater of Diamonds State Park has been there.

are found in the gravel, and the regulars bring screens, shovels, and buckets to pursue their dream. Visitors can rent the proper equipment for a small fee.

According to Hall, the largest diamond ever found by a visitor since the state took over the park was a 16.37-carat white diamond, called the Amarillo Starlight, discovered in 1975 by W. W. Johnson from Texas. After Johnson died, it is suspected his wife kept it.

The largest diamond unearthed at the site was a 40.23-carat gem uncovered in 1924. Named Uncle Sam, it is the largest diamond ever discovered in North America.

In 1956, rock hunter Winnie Parker found the 15.36-carat flawless gem called the Star of Arkansas. Cut into a marquis shape of 8.27 carats and set in a ring, it sold at Christie's auction house in New York City a few years ago for $145,000.

Then there is James Archer of Nashville, Arkansas, who holds the distinction as the most regular treasure hunter at the park. He's been steadfast in his search for over twenty years; day after day he's out there. He's found everything from specks up to a 5.50-carat yellow stone on July 19, 1994. It made the local and even national news, but it wasn't quite the "big one" he dreamed of because it wasn't a perfect gem and couldn't be cut. However, valuable yellow and also brown diamonds are found at the park.

Archer says of his diamond-hunting ability, "It's easy if you know how to do it." He doesn't have special secrets, but is referring to the normal procedure of putting the rocks and gravel on a screen and shaking it in water so the material will separate. Then the screen is removed from the water, and if a diamond is there, it will be more visible. He's quick to add, though, that he's out there because he enjoys the search. Archer's find was the biggest since 1991, when Murfreesboro resident Joe Fedzora found a 6.23-carat diamond. Hall says that Fedzora was asking $15,000 for it but doesn't know if it was sold.

Naturally, it isn't always the size of the diamond that makes it valuable, but the quality. Shirley Strawn of Murfreesboro, a regular at the park, had a dream come true. In October 1990 she unearthed a 3.03-carat white diamond that appeared to be flawless, but not until it was cut in 1998 did gemologists learn the exceptional quality of the stone.

Hall says that after the stone was cut in New York, the American Gem Society laboratory certified the diamond as "D" Flawless, 0/0/0 (for cut/color/clarity). This is based on the Gemological Institute of America scale.

Diamonds are graded on color and imperfections. "D" is

the grade given to a pure white stone that does not show any color at all and then the letters of the alphabet go on from there. The "0" shows that there are no imperfections of any kind.

Bill Underwood, who is a Fayetteville jeweler and certified gemologist appraiser, consulted with Strawn and her husband when they decided to have the diamond cut. He said in an interview, "A diamond of this exceptional quality is so rare that many gemologists and jewelers never see one. A diamond this perfect is one-in-ten-million." He adds that gems of this quality from diamond mines in Africa have exceeded $30,000 a carat, but because it was unearthed in Arkansas it could be much more valuable.

Strawn named her gem the "Strawn/Wagner Diamond" to honor her great-great-grandfather Lee Wagner, who worked at the site years before it became a state park in 1972. She said, "Because he worked there for over 40 years, I've always felt close to him in 'the field of shiny stones' as I call it."

Hall says that many people are hoping the diamond can be purchased by the state of Arkansas and kept at the park, since the family history is so involved with it and it would seem a shame to let it go. Meanwhile, Strawn has her diamond.

In 1998 there was a first for diamond hunting. On April 7, a mother and daughter visiting the park found a 7.28-carat pale yellow diamond, making it the fifth largest stone found by a visitor since the park opened. Hall says, "The diamond is about the size and shape of a lemon drop, and the first time in the park's history a mother and daughter made the find together." It was quite a surprise for them because at the time they didn't know what they had found was a diamond. After they finished their rockhounding an hour later, they showed the contents of their little brown sack to park officials to identify their finds. "The diamond immediately caught our eye," Hall said. "And we got to tell them the good news. This is the first time in my 15 years as park superintendent that a diamond of this size was totally unrecognized and unexpected by its 'finders.' "

He says that the diamond is gem quality and a cuttable stone, but the mother and daughter have not yet decided whether to have the gem cut and faceted, or to leave the diamond in its natural form.

Hall sees quite an array of devices used by the eager treasure hunters to uncover diamonds. "I saw a fellow with dowsing rods which were two probes that worked off a battery. He was hoping his rods would point to a spot where there were diamonds. The fascinating thing about this job is seeing people with all the different things and hopefully productive means of finding them."

Probably one of the more unusual methods for finding a diamond was used by logger George Stepp of Carthage, Arkansas, in 1978 when he found a flawless 4.25-carat yellow diamond at the park. He took home five 5-gallon buckets of stones and baked them in the oven. When that type of rock gets hot, it crumbles, and that's when Stepp found the diamond. He was told to take the diamond to Pine Bluff gemologist Stan Kahn because he was the only diamondologist in Arkansas at the time. Kahn sent it to New York to verify the stone and it was determined to be flawless.

An offer to buy came from someone who had done the diamond splitting in the old Mercury car commercial. Some years ago, the commercial was produced to show what a smooth ride the Mercury provided. To prove the point, a diamond cutter was seated in the backseat with a small table and tools in front of him. As the car was being driven at normal speed, the diamond cutter went into action and cut the stone perfectly.

Kahn thought it was important to keep the gem in Arkansas and not cut it because Arkansas is known as the "Natural State"—so he bought it. Kahn first placed the diamond in a pendant and then later in a specially designed ring. He is a good friend of the Clintons, and at Governor Clinton's first inaugural ball, Mrs. Clinton wore the pendant; at the second inaugural ball she wore the ring. Both Kahn and Mrs. Clinton felt pride in showing off the valuable gem found in their state. Kahn also loaned the ring to Mrs. Clinton to wear at President Clinton's first inaugural ball. Once again, she wanted to honor Arkansas by wearing the diamond.

Kahn has not placed a specific value on what has come to be known as the "Kahn Canary" because he has no plans to sell it.

While the eager are still out there sifting and sorting at Crater of Diamonds State Park, men needn't take that old adage "Diamonds are a girl's best friend" seriously. They are finding valuable diamonds and loving it.

CHAPTER 20

The Punch Jones Diamond

The Jones family had seventeen children, sixteen boys in a row and then a girl, which in itself is a treasure. But they found another one in their own backyard.

Grover C. Jones was born in West Virginia around 1890. As a young man he became a teacher in a one-room schoolhouse just across the state line in Virginia, where he continued to teach for forty-five years. In those days, the teacher often boarded with a local family, and Grover took up residence with the Bucklands at their farm in Giles County, Virginia.

One of the Buckland children, Annie, was also Grover's student at the school. Annie was ten years younger than Grover but once she graduated, they knew they had found true love. They were married and their first son, William P., nicknamed "Punch," was born in 1917. He was followed by fifteen brothers, a record for consecutive male births that still stands. In 1946, daughter Charlotte was born, but that's getting ahead of the story.

In 1921, the Jones family moved into their house in Peterstown, Monroe County, West Virginia, very near the Virginia border. Population was 300 at the time and has never exceeded 600. Punch and his father enjoyed pitching horseshoes in the backyard of their Peterstown home near the banks of Rich Creek. On a balmy Sunday afternoon in April 1928, they were outdoors pitching horseshoes when Punch went to pick up one he had thrown and saw that it was embedded in a foot-deep pit that errant throws had gouged out around the stake during the many games. When he dug out the horseshoe, it kicked up some dirt and he saw a brilliant glassy mass, about three-quarters of an inch in diameter. After picking it up, he jokingly called out to his father, "See, I have found a diamond."

Neither father nor son believed they had the real thing, but Grover thought he would keep the shiny piece of what he thought was probably quartz. Later that day he put it in a box with some odds and ends and tools in the shed. They both forgot about it, and the years passed.

The family faced great financial hardship during the Depression of the 1930s. By 1940 there were fifteen boys to feed, clothe, and educate. Grover and Annie believed strongly in education and wanted to be certain all their children would go on to college, rather unusual in an area where most men went to work in the coal mines. It was a constant struggle to find enough money just for necessities. Grover never made more than $77 per month, and even though the boys had various jobs, there were days when the situation seemed nearly hopeless.

The fame of the fifteen Jones boys (the sixteenth hadn't been born yet) spread outside Peterstown, and in 1940 the family was honored at the New York World's Fair with "Grover Jones Family Day." They were invited to the White House and had lunch with Mrs. Roosevelt because President Roosevelt was at a war meeting. The First Lady took the family on a tour of the White House, and "Tooter" Jones remembers sitting in the President's chair in the Oval Office. Postcards bearing the pictures of the parents and the fifteen boys in a row were printed, and pictures of the family were in newspapers around the country. Promoters tried to lure them into "showbiz" by offering "big money" and asked the family to tour the country. Tooter said that the offers were to endorse various products, and for this they would be paid hundreds of thousands of dollars. The money would have helped, but the parents had no desire to exploit their boys and allow them to be looked at as a sideshow attraction, so they declined all offers.

Punch was the first to fulfill his parents' dream, working his way through Concord College in Athens, West Virginia. After graduation he followed his father's example and became a teacher in a Monroe County school. At the beginning of World War II, he left his teaching job and went to work at the nearby Radford Arsenal, an army ammunitions plant, where he worked with carbons. Since diamonds are crystallized carbon, his work made him think of the shiny rock he had found years before. Even though it was farfetched to think it was a diamond, why not check it out?

Punch asked his father to find it, and at first Grover couldn't remember where he had put it nearly fifteen years before. Eventually he remembered it was probably out in the toolshed somewhere, but the question was, where? Grover searched through all sorts of things piled out there and, after nearly giving up hope, finally found the box with the rock inside.

Punch wanted to have it tested by R. J. Holden, a noted geology professor at Virginia Polytechnic Institute in Blacksburg, not far away from Peterstown. First he decided to conduct his own test and see if the stone would scratch glass, knowing a diamond is the hardest known substance. The ninth-born son, W. W. "Tooter" Jones, now a retired school principal and about five years old at the time, remembers the day. "Punch took the stone and pressed the edge of it across the window and it left a big scratch. He was excited when that happened because a diamond cuts glass."

This is a copy of the letter Punch sent to Professor Holden, May 5, 1943:

Dear Sir:

This is to accompany a crystal which I am herewith delivering to you for identification and study.

This was found in April 1928, in a vacant lot at my home in Peterstown, where my father, Grover C. Jones, and I were pitching horseshoes. The point of discovery—on land owned by my father—was near the main street on a short street, which diverges from the main street and on the flood-plain of Rich creek about twenty-five feet from the stream. Games of horseshoes had gouged a hole about a foot deep below the surface. At one cast the horseshoe rang and a bright object was disclosed in the hole. On digging this out, it proved to be a rounded, faceted, glassy mass of striking brilliance about 3/4 inch in diameter. With boyish imagination I said, "See, I have found a diamond." The improbability of this optimistic statement prevented a serious consideration of the idea, but the exceptional character of the stone caused it to be retained as a curio. I did not submit this for study because I did not care to face ridicule for my wild suspicion.

About a year ago I started reading about natural crystals of diamond and to compare my stone with published descriptions. I learned that diamond has a low affinity for water, less than that of any of its imitations. A small drop of water on the cleaned surface of my crystal did not spread but tended to round up.

I now request your opinion on this crystal.

Very truly yours,
William P. Jones

Tooter Jones says that Professor Holden was at first reluctant to see the stone because so many people had come to him through the years claiming they had diamonds and none of the stones had been the real thing. However, the professor did take the stone from Punch and ran some tests. He sent this reply, dated also May 5, 1943.

Dear Sir:

This is in reply to your letter of May 5, asking for my opinion on the crystal accompanying your letter.

After a study of this stone it is my opinion that this is a diamond. It is the largest one ever found in the eastern United States, a third larger than the largest previous find, the Dewey diamond, and one of the largest ever found in North America. It is of good color and appears to be comparatively free from imperfections. A more detailed discus-

sion is being prepared, which with your approval I will offer for publication.

Very truly yours,
R. J. HOLDEN Professor of Geology

Tooter Jones remembers going to Blacksburg several times with Punch and the diamond so that Holden could run more tests. Eventually the professor wrote a long paper on the diamond, which was published and read by many geologists. He also suggested that the 34.46-carat gem be sent to the Smithsonian Institution in Washington, D.C., because of its uniqueness. The family agreed to allow the diamond to be displayed there, and beginning in 1944 the Punch Jones Diamond was placed near the famous Hope Diamond.

The Punch Jones Diamond, the only diamond to be found in the state of West Virginia.

In 1945 Punch Jones went into the army and trained at Camp Fannin, Texas. He was sent overseas in February 1945, landing in France and later moving into Germany with the 97th Infantry Division. On Easter Sunday, April 1, 1945, Punch Jones was killed in action in Germany seventeen years after that other Sunday in April when he found the diamond that would forever bear his name.

Altogether, six Jones brothers served in World War II and five in the Korean War, in all branches of the service. Four were wounded and between them received four Purple Hearts, one Bronze Star, and various other honors. They had a legacy of military service since their great-great-grandfather was killed in the Revolutionary War, their great-grandfather was killed in the War of 1812, their grandfather seriously wounded in the Civil War, and their father, Grover, was called up in World War I but fortunately for him the war ended before he had to go.

While the sixteen brothers and one sister grew up, attended college, married, had children and went through heartache and happiness, the Punch Jones Diamond remained on display at the Smithsonian. Then in 1968 the family decided it was time to bring it home, and it was shown at the state fair. Later, that unique diamond, the only one to be found in West Virginia, was placed in a safe deposit box in the Rich Creek Bank. A historical marker was placed on the spot where twelve-year-old Punch had found the diamond.

After Grover C. Jones died in 1973 at eighty-five, the ownership of the diamond was then shared by Punch's mother, Annie, and his only son, Robert Jones. In 1984, Robert sold the diamond through Sotheby's auction house in

New York for nearly $80,000 to an unidentified buyer from the Orient. Annie received $40,000 for her share.

Where did the diamond come from? That will always remain a mystery, but many experts believe glaciers in the Ice Age deposited the isolated diamonds in the United States.

Annie died at age ninety-three in 1993. In a 1990 interview in *The Roanoke Times,* she said she didn't regret that the diamond had left the family because it was never more than a novelty and certainly much less novel than raising seventeen children. "To me, the diamond wasn't a big deal. It was nothing more than holding a rock in your hand."

Tooter Jones speaks with pride about the accomplishments of his siblings. Of the eleven who went to various colleges and universities, three earned doctorates, and Tooter himself boasts a master's. Before he retired, he was a teacher, guidance counselor, and school principal. Seven other siblings are still living and became successful in law, business, and education—one was a college dean and another, a high school principal.

It seems that the real legacy of the Punch Jones Diamond was not wealth or notoriety, but the accomplishments of those many children who honored their parents' love of learning. It was a true treasure to prove the American Dream.

CHAPTER 21

MEL FISHER AND THE *ATOCHA*

The name Mel Fisher has come to be synonymous with the word *treasure* because of his legendary search for the sunken Spanish galleon *Atocha.* It took him more than sixteen years to find the ship that would bring him both terrible tragedy and the thrill of discovery.

Fisher grew up in Glen Park, Indiana, certainly nowhere near the sea that would become so much a part of his life. After reading Robert Louis Stevenson's *Treasure Island* as a child and stories of pirates of the Spanish Main, he was captivated by the thought of finding treasure. By age eleven, the stories he read about the exploits of deep-sea divers, who in those days were wearing their bulky "hard hat" suits to explore the undersea world, prompted him to make his own first "hard hat" diving outfit. Fisher couldn't go out to sea in it, so he settled for the next best thing, a local mud-bottomed lagoon.

In addition to treasure, Fisher loved music and played the saxophone and clarinet. In high school he formed his first dance band. Then, at Purdue University where he studied engineering, he led his own twenty-one-piece band. When World War II began, Fisher went into the army and after training served with the U.S. Army Corps of Engineers. Before they were sent to Europe, he studied at the University of Alabama. When the war ended, Fisher lived for a time in Chicago and then Denver, before the lure of the sea and his love of diving took him to Florida. There, he saw his first real treasure from a sunken ship.

Always innovative, Fisher made spearguns, cameras, and other equipment necessary for him to pursue his dream. When he heard that Jacques Cousteau had perfected an underwater breathing unit, called the Aqua-Lung, Fisher drove to California so he would be among the first to have one. The device then became known as scuba (self-contained underwater breathing apparatus), and the words *scuba diving* became part of the language.

Then, as luck would have it, Fisher's parents moved to Torrance, California, to open a chicken ranch. He could not only work with them but was near the ocean and could also pursue his love of diving. He opened a shop on the family property, where he had a small compressor: a first. He was able to sell "breathing" air and scuba equipment to divers.

The sale of the family's enterprise changed his life, for it allowed him to meet red-haired Dolores Horton when her mother and uncle bought the ranch. Soon Mel and Dolores were married. It seemed an unusual match at first because Dolores was from Montana and had no knowledge of or interest in the ocean. That soon changed, and on their honeymoon they went diving on shipwrecks in Florida and the Florida Keys. Dolores eventually became known as "Deo," a new name to go along with her new life.

To raise the money needed to open what would be the first "dive shop" in the world, Mel and Deo dove commercially for spiny lobsters found in cold California waters. It wasn't easy, but the effort paid off. They were able to build their shop one wall at a time until finally Mel's Aqua Shop in Redondo Beach, California, was a reality. They were pioneers, teaching scuba diving to more than 65,000 eager novices. It was at this time that Deo set a world underwater endurance record for women that has never been broken. It was fifty-five hours and thirty-seven minutes or, to be exact, 55:37:9.6 underwater with scuba equipment. They were then and have remained an incomparable couple and were the unofficial "king and queen" of the underwater world. Their four children—sons Dirk, Kim, and Kane, and daughter Taffi—literally grew up in the water and were always part of the family's endeavors.

For a time Mel hunted for gold in California's mountains and streams, but always on his mind were those golden doubloons of Spanish shipwrecks. Appropriately, his first dive boat was named the *Golden Doubloon.*

The Fishers began diving for shipwrecks off the California coast and then tried their luck in the Caribbean. They did not have great success, but the experience they gained was important for the future. Then, in 1963, Mel met Kip Wagner in Florida. Wagner and some friends had been trying to salvage treasure from the wrecks of the 1715 Spanish Plate Fleet lost off the east coast of Florida. Wagner could not commit full-time to the project, so he invited Mel to join him and they worked out a financial arrangement.

Mel and Deo decided to move to Florida, where they began the very difficult diving on the 1715 fleet shipwrecks. Because the ships had gone down close to shore, the water was too murky to provide much visibility. Dr. Fay Field, an electronics wizard and a member of the team, developed a sensitive device called a proton magnetometer that was able to find portions of those elusive ships by signaling the presence of iron. If there was an anchor, cannon, or cannonball, it indicated that a ship was nearby. However, the fact that they couldn't see in shallow water was still hampering their efforts. Fisher put his engineering skills to work and developed a device they called a "mailbox" because of its shape. It was lowered from the salvage ship's stern over the propellers, then sent a layer of clear water downward from the surface to the bottom so the divers could see. Near the end of 1964, Mel had an unforgettable experience. By parting the sands at the bottom of the sea, the "mailbox" allowed 1,033 gold coins to become visible. Fisher has often been quoted with the words he said at the time: "Once you have seen the ocean bottom paved with gold, you'll never forget it!"

During the 1960s the Fisher team of Treasure Salvors, Inc., with the Wagner team of the Real Eight Company, recovered more than $20 million in treasure from the 1715 fleet shipwrecks. Those shipwrecks are still being salvaged and have produced even more treasure through the years, with no end in sight.

By the mid-sixties Fisher realized that because of the weather and winter storms along the east coast of Florida, he couldn't dive year-round, so he began to search for shipwrecks in the calmer waters off the Florida Keys. Perhaps it was always meant to be, but no matter the reason, Fisher renewed his interest in an unsalvaged sunken Spanish galleon that was said to be possibly the richest ever lost off the coast of Florida. It was called the *Nuestra Señora de Atocha* and was believed to have gone down in 1622 off the Matecumbe Keys of Florida.

Around 1968, Fisher met history teacher Eugene Lyon in church in Vero Beach, Florida, and they became friends. When he learned that Lyon was going to the Archive of the Indies in Seville, Spain, to do research for his doctorate in Spanish-American history, it was another one of those fateful happenings. Fisher told him about the *Atocha* and where it was supposed to have gone down. He asked Lyon to do some research on the ship while at the archive, since the Spanish kept meticulous records of all their ships coming from and going to the New World. Lyon's excellent research showed that the *Atocha* was much farther south than others had supposed. He learned that the Spanish referred to all of the keys as Matecumbe Keys, because of Matecumbe Island near Key Largo. That is why others had placed the *Atocha* in the area. Lyon found that instead of being off Key Largo, where most people thought it would be, the *Atocha* was actually about thirty miles off Key West in what is now known as the Bermuda Triangle.

With the new information, Fisher began his search for the *Atocha* in 1968. He said, "We searched 200,000 miles of ocean back and forth for two years before we saw the first signs of the *Atocha*."

On September 4, 1622, the *Atocha* was one of the escort galleons in a fleet of twenty-eight ships that left Havana Harbor, bringing treasures of the New World home to Spain, where the gold, silver, and jewels were badly needed to bolster the economy. Although Spain was the most powerful European nation at the time, more and more wealth was needed to maintain the king, his court, and his armies.

In Dr. Eugene Lyon's book, *The Search for the* Atocha (Harper & Row), he wrote: "The wealth in the holds of the 1622 fleet represented 'private savings and royal extravagance, swollen profits and pious gifts, the fruits of injustice and the hope of Heaven.' "

The ships sailed directly into the path of a devastating hurricane, but amazingly, twenty-two ships survived. The *Atocha* struck a shallow reef and settled in 55 feet of water. Five crew members managed to survive, but 260 others, mainly passengers, were lost. Another of the escort galleons, the *Santa Margarita,* ended up 3 miles away on a wide shoal known as the Quicksands. Again, 68 crewmen survived, but none of the 120 passengers. The survivors of the ships were able to later give their eyewitness accounts of the sinkings.

When Fisher began his search, the *Atocha* had been at the bottom of the sea with all her treasure for nearly 350 years, and he was sure he would find it. Throughout his hunt for treasure, Fisher would optimistically say, "Today's the day."

Fisher soon found that portions of the elusive ship and treasure had washed over a 10-mile expanse of sea bottom. He began finding gold bars that matched the manifest. "We found the serial numbers and name of the mint on the gold bars so we knew they were from the *Atocha*," Fisher said.

Then, in 1975, tragedy struck when Mel and Deo's first-born son, Dirk, his wife, Angel, and another diver, all part of the team searching for the *Atocha,* drowned in a boating accident.

Mel Fisher and *Atocha* treasure, Mel Fisher photo courtesy of Pat Clyne

***Treasure hunter Mel Fisher, displaying some of the treasure he recovered from the* Atocha.**

It was nearly impossible for Fisher to go on, but he persevered. They had to find the Mother Lode where the majority of the treasure would be found.

It was 1:05 P.M. on July 20, 1985, when Fisher, in his Treasure Salvors, Inc., Key West office, heard the crackling of the marine radio and his son Kane's voice: "WZG 9605. Unit 1, this is Unit 11. You can put away the charts now. We've got the Mother Lode!"

It was a bittersweet victory because of their tragic personal loss, but Fisher had done something that others throughout history had only imagined. Now the world would see the stacks of silver bars, gold in many forms, emeralds, and chests of treasure coins as well as unusual artifacts. All those who scoffed through the years, and many did, would have to acknowledge that Mel Fisher had really done it. It wasn't a pipedream!

Throughout the search Fisher had to deal with investors and the seemingly endless court battle with the state of Florida for salvage rights. Finally after many years of litigation, a Supreme Court victory gave him the rights. A brilliant young attorney, David Paul Horan, successfully prosecuted the case for him, which led Horan to an illustrious career in maritime law.

The treasure was divided among the delighted investors, but more had to be done. It would take years to salvage all the treasure on the *Atocha* because Fisher estimated that the $400 million in treasure found was only 20 percent of the tons of gold, silver, and thousands of emeralds aboard.

Fisher was always careful to work with archaeologists and professional treasure conservators so that everything would be properly cared for and documented, not only for investors but for the cultural and historical heritage of the world. Even before he found the *Atocha,* he had established a small museum in Key West. However, with some of the proceeds of the *Atocha* he bought a spacious former Key West naval station and opened the nonprofit Mel Fisher Maritime Heritage Society Museum. The museum houses treasures found on various ships as well as a research center and conservation laboratories.

In the 1990s the Mel Fisher Center, Inc., was opened in Sebastian, Florida, to exhibit and conserve new finds from the 1715 fleet. Daughter Taffi is in charge of this museum, while son Kane continues the search for treasure at several locations and Kim takes care of the business end of treasure.

The *Atocha* hasn't yet given up all its treasures. The salvage will continue into the next millennium, Fisher predicted. He said, "It's a big ocean out there. There's a couple of billion in emeralds still on the *Atocha* going by the rough-cut price. I figure if we're lucky we'll get done by the year 2000."

Although the *Atocha* was the heart of Fisher's operations, he was searching twenty-three different wreck sites.

He said, "I keep going because I really enjoy it." And he did keep going until cancer stopped him on December 19, 1998, at age seventy-six. The world has lost a real gem. A one-of-a-kind person who will always be remembered for the amazing treasures he found—but probably the more important treasure was his eternal optimism and his motto with words that should be an inspiration to everyone: "Today's the day!"

CHAPTER 22

The 1715 Fleet

Even kings need money, and this was the case of Philip V of Spain in 1715. Wars were raging on many fronts, so he ordered his treasure ships in from the New World.

Heeding the king's urgent decree, a fleet set sail from Havana Harbor at sunrise on July 24, their hulls and stern-castles packed full of treasure. On the sixth day of their voyage, luck ran out when a violent hurricane sank the twelve ships. The entire fleet was gone, three in deep water and the rest closer to shore up and down the wild and untamed eastern coast of Florida, from St. Augustine south to what is now Cape Canaveral.

The 1715 fleet has a unique distinction because it spawned a breed of determined dreamers who would find exceptional riches and fame. Salvage work on the ships has been done by nearly every great treasure hunter. It is as though they cut their teeth on it and the experience helped lead them to their great successes ahead, as happened to Mel Fisher and the *Atocha*, and to Bob Marx and the *Maravilla*. They blazed a trail for the others.

The fleet lay untouched and unknown until 1955, when building contractor Kip Wagner took a walk along the beach of Sebastian, Florida. He stopped to look at some objects that had washed ashore and thought they were seashells, but quite unusual shells. He decided to scrape off the coating of one of the darkened objects and discovered that what he had were not seashells, but silver pieces of eight. Wagner did some research and realized he had found treasure from one of the sunken galleons of the ill-fated 1715 fleet.

He formed the Real Eight Company, which would eventually become the first group of full-time treasure hunters. Among the members were his nephew Rex Stocker, and a group of divers who were officers and civilians stationed at nearby Patrick Air Force Base: Del Long, Colonel Dan Thompson, Lou Ullian, and Colonel Harry Cannon.

At first they were part-time treasure hunters, but some of the coins and other artifacts were so close to shore and in such shallow water that there were days when they could go out with snorkels and garden rakes and bring in hundreds of silver coins.

Around 1960, Wagner contacted Bob Marx, who was living in Spain at the time and already had quite a reputation as a treasure hunter and marine archaeologist. Wagner asked Marx to do research on the fleet at the Archive of the Indies in Seville, where records were kept of all the treasure ships. This was Marx's first involvement with the 1715 fleet. He gathered a great deal of information on it and learned that there had been some survivors from the ships that were close to shore. Their firsthand accounts of the disaster helped the salvors find some of the wrecks. At this time, Marx only provided research on the 1715 fleet. He did not work on salvaging any of those wrecks because he was pursuing other sunken ships.

Then, in 1963, Mel Fisher became involved when Wagner asked him to join, and Real Eight began operating as a full-time salvage company. Fisher also brought to the group Mo Molinar, an exceptional treasure hunter he had met in Panama. By 1967, Bob Marx arrived on the scene to run four salvage boats for Real Eight and three others for Mel Fisher.

By 1972, Mel Fisher was diligently pursuing the *Atocha* and Bob Marx, the *Maravilla.* The Real Eight Company experienced financial problems and they decided to sell to a group headed by former race car driver and Indianapolis winner Jim Rathman, who had a car dealership in Melbourne, Florida, next to Cape Canaveral. Other members of the company, which became known as Circle Bar Salvage of Louisiana, included astronaut Gus Grissom, who was tragically killed during a launchpad accident; John Meacham, who owned the New Orleans Saints; and Ed Cole, a General Motors executive who was later killed in a plane crash. Treasure certainly attracts a diverse group of enthusiasts.

Marx remained involved with that group and then bought it from them in 1981. He then divided the wrecks with Mel Fisher, and the six wrecks that have been found are actively being salvaged by a number of subcontractors who are professional treasure hunters. Wagner no longer had an involvement with the 1715 fleet, but several others continued to work on it through the years. John Brandon, one of these subcontractors, has been working on the 1715 fleet for more

Coins and jewelry recovered from the 1715 fleet.

than twenty-eight years. He began his treasure career at age sixteen with Mel Fisher, and has recovered hundreds of thousands of dollars in gold, silver, and jewels.

Many factors seduced Brandon into the treasure-seeking game: an appreciation for history, a love of the beauty and art of the treasure itself, and the lure of gold. "Gold shines forever," he says, "it just takes your breath away." He is always excited when he sees various treasures. "When you first pick the things up, you wonder about the last people to touch them. What thoughts they had in their minds when the ship was breaking up around them. A day or so before they were wealthy and probably happy then suddenly, they would have given up everything to get themselves out of the predicament they were in, the sinking ship."

Wagner wasn't the only treasure hunter to profit off the 1715 fleet. Harold Holden has also been successfully salvaging treasure from it for many years. Among his finds have been a gold locket at the end of a 10-foot-long braided gold chain valued at $850,000 and a gold box or picture holder with filigree doors valued at $1.5 million. Many of these unusual and valuable items are in Mel Fisher's museums.

It was Holden's discovery of a gold sword hilt in 1987 that led to a mutual effort by him, Brandon, and Molinar that proved to be as elusive as it was amazing. Because they had all found gold coins in the area of the sword hilt, they realized they had hit upon a trail of coins about 50 feet wide and half a mile long. It took all their expertise and the use of modern technology to pursue a trail that, as they said, "was so narrow and so thin." Finally, together they found eight hundred gold coins worth $2.5 million.

The difficulty involved in the discovery prompted Brandon to say, "If it was easy, everybody would be out there doing it."

There are times however, when it does appear to be easy. Chris James, a florist from Palm Beach whose family had invested in the company salvaging the treasure, had permission to go out to the wreck sites. In 1993, with metal detector in hand, he went out on Bob and Margaret Weller's boat to a site they had been working. The Wellers are successful professional treasure hunters who are subcontractors for Mel Fisher.

"I was swimming along the edge of the reef and I heard a faint signal from the detector so I started digging," he said. "Suddenly some gold came out and I was so excited I started to shriek so loud I thought they could hear me out of the water." He had good reason to shriek: He had found two gold and diamond brooches. One had 170 diamonds and the other, 144 diamonds. The combined value of the two was a million dollars.

Marx says that one of the wrecks near Frederick Douglass Beach has produced the most coins, yet on the original manifest there is no mention of anything of value. As he has often said, "There was always contraband on those ships." He estimates that from the time the first coins were found by Kip Wagner to the present, at least $100 million in treasure has been salvaged and some of the gold coins are worth more each year. "Remember, only six ships have been found so far. There's millions more in treasure out there." To which Holden adds, "They'll be finding it for many years to come."

Next time you walk along a Florida beach, or any beach, look carefully at those shifting sands. You, too, might just find a treasure.

CHAPTER 23

GEM MOUNTAIN

A North Carolina man was walking along a road one day and noticed an odd-shaped crystal. It turned out to be a gem so valuable, he traded it for an island.

The gem that was found wasn't an isolated incident, for North Carolina, specifically Mitchell County, is the gem capital of the United States. One can find rubies, sapphires, emeralds, and at least twenty other gem varieties in those Blue Ridge Mountains. Even though most gems come from exotic places such as Thailand, Burma, and Brazil, the famous Tiffany jewelers came to mine their own emeralds in North Carolina.

Anyone can go prospecting at the Gem Mountain mine in Spruce Pine. It began thirty years ago when retired real estate agent Bill Collins bought the former Tiffany mine and opened it to the public. His daughter, Helen Woody, said, "People paid $4.00 to get in and sometimes left with hundreds of thousands of dollars' worth of gems. To my father, the emeralds were more valuable the way they were found, the way nature made them. He thought they were more beautiful in the rock than to have them cut. He was always happy when somebody else found the emeralds, just as happy as if he found them himself. He just loved the emeralds." Woody often shows some of her father's emeralds in the rock. One is valued at $7,000, and another at $5,000.

At the time Collins owned the mine there were seven hundred in the area. They produced feldspar and mica, and the gemstones just happened to be along for the ride. Feldspar is used in pottery and porcelain. Mica, like feldspar a dustlike material, was used to make the capacitor essential to filter signals in electronic circuits.

Charles Buchanan's father was a miner in those lovely green hills, and Charles often went along with him, picking up stones in the mines. When he was grown, he started several mines, and with the money from the stones he harvested from them, he bought the Collins mine and turned it into Gem Mountain, where people find not only emeralds but a variety of stones. He said, "Mica once sold for $400 a pound but when business went to other countries it wasn't profitable for us so we turned to gems." Many of the mines closed.

The motto at Gem Mountain is "You buy 'em, you keep 'em." Prices for a bucket of rocks run from $7 to $100. The prices vary according to the size of the bucket, and the $100 bucket entitles the buyer to have two stones cut free—ordinarily the fee is $40 to have a stone cut so that it can be used in a ring or other jewelry. Buchanan said that people almost always find something. Buckets of rocks are brought from his other mines in the area, and this provides the variety of stones. People hunt for and find emeralds, rubies, sapphires, amethysts, aquamarines, and many other varieties of jewels. The rocks are placed on a screen and run through water. People match the stones to a color chart and then have them checked by experts at the mine.

One regular at Gem Mountain is Mr. Batchelor, who has found a total of $140,000 worth of various gems. Another steady treasure hunter is Bette Cain, who has rings, pendants, and earrings made from gemstones she has found at the mine. Her most amazing find was in 1995, when she had a rock she thought looked like a red potato. When she brought it in to be identified, she was shocked to learn that she had a 672-carat ruby that would cut into two good stones. Together they would be worth at least $36,000.

Residents of the area find gems in their own backyards. James and Sandra Hite were putting up a wall at their home in 1986. While they were doing some excavating they found a large stone in the exposed ground. It turned out to be a very good aquamarine, which would cut into two stones worth $20,000 together. Aquamarines can run from $600 to $3,000 a carat.

Buchanan said, "To look for treasure you have to be some sort of a gambler. It's always a gamble. You'll always be gambling. You'll find that big stone, that treasure, a great stone." He found his treasure one day as he was walking down the road, but didn't know what he had found. It turned out to be a star sapphire. After cutting, it was 466 carats, and he wound up trading it for an island in Florida. He plans to build a vacation home there one day, but his heart is always in North Carolina, his real treasure.

Charles Buchanan, owner of Gem Mountain, eyeing a large aquamarine.

If you're in North Carolina, keep your eyes on the ground. You, too, could find a treasure. Of course, you can head for Gem Mountain and boost your chances of taking home a valuable keepsake.

CHAPTER 24

The Rembrandt Plate

A famous painter's work of art disappeared for more than three hundred years, then reappeared in an unlikely place.

In 1997 a woman who wishes to remain anonymous went to Christie's auction house in London to have a painting of a landscape appraised. She hoped it would be worth selling and waited expectantly for the opinion of the art expert. Dr. Liesbeth Heenk, Rembrandt print specialist at Christie's, was asked to examine the painting because it was done by Flemish artist Pieter Gysels (1620–90), a contemporary of Rembrandt's.

Heenk removed the frame of the painting to examine it in more detail. She was amazed and delighted when she recognized on the reverse of the painting a copperplate etched by Rembrandt. The Gysels painting had been done on the copper, a common practice at the time. The Rembrandt etching was used to make prints of the original.

The Rembrandt plate, © Christie's Images, London

The Rembrandt plate, discovered on the reverse side of a painting by Pieter Gysels.

Heenk said, "I examined the copperplate and immediately recognized it as a Rembrandt. This plate was used for one of the most superb of Rembrandt's etchings. Of all plates known to us, this one is certainly in the best condition as it was never reworked after his death. This discovery represents a unique addition to the plates known to us. The fact that Pieter Gysels made a landscape on the reverse makes the plate a very exciting historic document. It is a profoundly exciting discovery and an important addition to our knowledge of the working methods of this artist."

The print tells the story of Abraham and the Angels from

Genesis 18:1–15, where the Lord appears to Abraham in the guise of three men. Abraham, who offers them food and drink, is being told that his elderly wife Sarah will bear a son. Rembrandt has placed the group in front of a substantial house with an arched doorway. Sarah overhears the revelation in stunned disbelief. Ishmael, Abraham's son by Sarah's Egyptian maid Hagar, is playing with his bow and arrow in the background.

The woman who owned the painting was even more shocked than Dr. Heenk. Her family bought the oil painting in 1946, at an antique shop in Yorkshire. She said, "My family has always enjoyed the painting and admired the work of the artist, but imagine my amazement when it was divulged that there was a Rembrandt original hidden on the reverse. I was stunned when Christie's told me of the discovery. We had no idea."

How the plate was acquired by Gysels remains a mystery. Heenk said that it seems the plate was not used after 1656, the year it was cut, because research shows that prints from the original are unknown after that time. Rembrandt may have disposed of it that year because he had serious financial problems and was declared bankrupt. In an inventory of his possessions, drawn up at the time of his bankruptcy, none of his plates are mentioned. They would have been considered part of his working capital unless they were too severely damaged to be used. It has been suggested that Rembrandt purposely kept his plates out of the proceedings by pawning them or hiding them with friends.

It just proves once more that great talent doesn't necessarily bring riches. Rembrandt's etchings were quite popular during his lifetime, and when he ran out of stock of a particular print, he would often make reprints from his plates.

After Rembrandt's death his prints were still popular. To fill the orders for more impressions, most of the plates were reworked and restored by print dealers and publishers. Worn areas were strengthened, and some were altered to suit the fashion of the day. Because of careless reworking, some plates lost their original appearance.

Heenk said, "This plate is remarkable because it has never been reworked or rebitten [reetched]. It is by the hand of the master and reveals the mastery of his technique."

The next order of business was to set a date for the auction. The owner of the painting and then the unexpected plate was delighted to learn that instead of the painting she had hoped to sell, she now had a real treasure. Heenk said that the painting was worth around $5,000, but placed the value of the plate at $60,000 for opening bids at auction.

On June 26, 1997, Rembrandt's copperplate of Abraham entertaining the Angels was sold for £210,500, or $350,272, more than five times its presale estimate.

Heenk, who was thrilled with the results of the sale, said, "The atmosphere in the auction room was electric as bidders competed fiercely in the room and on the telephones. We had many bids to begin with, but finally it was between two determined people, one an anonymous lady bidder in the room competing with a client on the telephone. When the hammer came down, the lady in the room was the successful buyer."

Although the seller and buyer of the amazing and unexpected plate have remained anonymous, the description of the sale by the equally ecstatic Heenk summed up their feelings.

The moral of this story is that the back can be more valuable than the front. Turn that painting over, even though you think it's worthless!

CHAPTER 25

THE FABULOUS TABLE

A couple who lived in Connecticut had a table for thirty years and never realized it was a great American treasure.

The wife, a gray-haired woman in her seventies we shall call Joan, since she prefers to remain anonymous, purchased her claw-foot tea table for $180 from a decorator, who had found it in an antique store in Seattle, Washington. Joan loved it, and enjoyed using the table in her living room throughout the years. In the 1980s a neighbor told Joan she thought the table might be an old and valuable American antique. Joan was skeptical, but decided to do some research at the library. There she saw a picture of a table that appeared to be similar. It was a Goddard–Townsend tea table that was in a collection of American antiques established by Henry Du Pont at Winterthur in Delaware.

Joan briefly thought her table might be valuable, but really couldn't believe she had a true treasure. She wanted to

The Goddard–Townsend tea table.

have it checked by experts, and being a diligent researcher, she found the best place to go was Israel Sack and Company in New York City.

Israel Sack, Inc. and Company is the foremost firm in the world dealing in American antiques. It was founded in the early part of the century by Israel Sack, an immigrant from Eastern Europe. He would take his son Harold (now in his late eighties and still vibrant) around with him while he scoured antique stores in New England and the East Coast. Sometimes he paid a few dollars for a table or chair or some other piece of furniture that he thought would be valuable. Through the years the piece would be sold and resold, until at some point Israel Sack, and later his sons, would buy back a table or chair for hundreds of thousands of dollars and then sell it for even more. Some of their clients were Henry Ford, Rockefeller family members, Du Ponts, Jackie Kennedy Onassis, and many other major collectors whose names are not as well known to the public.

Albert Sack, the younger son, is also in his eighties and is a charming, talkative person whose entire life has been devoted to finding American antique treasures. He has seen a number of items that were in the homes of people who had purchased them for very little money, only to find out later that a table or chair was worth thousands or hundreds of thousands of dollars. He said, "Sometimes the furniture was bought and sold quite a few times before it reached many thousands."

The Sack brothers can trace the history of many pieces, and their stories give people hope that they might have something of value in their living room or even the attic. However, Albert said, "Some things should be left in the attic."

Joan contacted the firm and when she brought in a photo of her table and showed it to Harold Sack, he suggested it would be worthy of a museum, not an attic. Joan told him she thought it was similar to a Goddard table she had seen in a library book. That table was sold during the Depression to Henry Du Pont for $29,000, a huge amount at that time. Du Pont put it in his great antique collection at Winterthur in Delaware.

Goddard and Townsend were two Quakers who became known as superb artistic craftsmen. In their shop in Providence, Rhode Island, in the mid-1700s, they had a unique design on their tables. It was a ball-and-claw foot, which proved to be very popular in the United States and England at the time. The design varied from one area to another. Antique experts could recognize one of the Goddard–Townsend tables by the difference in the way the feet were carved.

In the 1930 table purchased by Du Pont the talons were open and one could see through the space. Harold Sack said that the carving was very beautiful and extremely rare. There were only three tables from 1750 to 1760 with that type of carving. Two were in Winterthur and one was in a private collection in Providence. There were also three other versions of the table where the claws on the foot were not open. Basically, the Sack brothers knew of only six tables with claw feet from Goddard–Townsend. They could hardly believe Joan's picture showed that her table was the "real thing," but if it was, the picture would mean there was a seventh table.

Albert and Harold Sack discussed the table. They felt the chances of its authenticity were slim, but they had learned through the years to not turn their backs on items that could be valuable. Albert went to see the table. He was amazed when he saw it because, against all odds, Joan really did have the seventh Goddard–Townsend tea table. Even more impressive, it was a previously unknown, fourth table with the intricate open ball-and-claw feet.

Albert Sack told Joan he would pay a good price for the table. He didn't set a specific amount and told Joan to think about it since she loved the table and didn't know if she really wanted to part with it.

When they had not heard from Joan for two weeks, the Sack brothers called her and were told she had decided to put the table up for auction with another company. Harold asked if he could come to discuss the matter with her and, of course, see the table himself. Joan agreed, and when Harold saw the table, he was thrilled to see it was just as Albert had described it, certainly authentic. He was able to convince Joan and her husband that after he bought it, he would sell it to someone who would cherish it and most likely leave it to a museum. Joan had a sentimental attachment to the table and wanted it to end up in a museum if she wasn't going to keep it. She said she would miss her table very much, but finally she and her husband agreed to Harold's price. Joan sold her table for $350,000. Harold paid such a high price because there were so few of those tables in existence, and he had been given a rare opportunity to buy one.

When the table arrived at Israel Sack, Inc., Harold and Albert had it checked by a man who was writing a book on the Goddard–Townsend furniture. He discovered it was the only open-talon, ball-and-claw-foot table carved by John Townsend. None other of that form had ever been located. The Sack brothers now owned one of the rarest pieces of early American furniture they had ever seen. They sold it to collectors, who love the table and keep it in their home. The table has been shown at the National Gallery in Washington, D.C.

Albert Sack recently said that the table is now worth over a million dollars.

Next time you think this could never happen to you, look carefully at your furniture. Anything is possible in the world of treasure.

CHAPTER 26

METEORITE MAN

He has a moon rock and a piece of Mars. No, he isn't an astronaut, he's Robert Haag, also known as Meteorite Man.

While some wait in fear for meteorites to fall and destroy the earth, this Tucson, Arizona, space age entrepreneur can't wait for the next one. To him, they are just as much treasure from above as gold and precious jewels are to those who search underground. The fact is that every two hours a softball-size meteorite hits the earth and thousands rain down in small particles, making Haag very happy and wealthy.

He has bought, sold, and traded millions of dollars' worth of meteorites. It is a unique market because demand always exceeds supply. Haag puts ads in publications geared to rock collectors or would-be astronomers. He is asking to buy and offering to sell meteorites. People in various parts of the world contact him with information about important finds. His motto is "Have cash, will travel anywhere in the world to make a deal." Filled with the spirit of adventure, he has gone from tiny, remote villages in little-known countries to the largest institutional collections. Now in his early forties, this upbeat man who looks like a rock star, with shoulder-length curly blond hair, is not shy about success. He feels he is the best in his field.

At times meteorites make quite an impact when they arrive on earth. Haag would like to have witnessed some of these events, such as the time in 1992 when a twenty-six-pound fragment crashed onto the trunk of a Chevy Malibu car in Peekskill, New York, while the owner was sitting in the house watching television. The meteorite was sold for $69,000 by the owner, who also sold her car to a collector. It was valued at $300 and was purchased for more than $10,000.

Haag's hunt for these amazing treasures began at an early age. His parents were rockhounds and ran a small shop in Tucson, Arizona. He and his brother and sister went along with their parents on prospecting trips. After witnessing a meteorite shower over the desert when he was eleven, Haag was hooked on rocks from the sky rather than those on the ground. This led him to become a geology major at the University of Arizona, eventually leaving school before graduation to work in a series of odd jobs. Always creative, he devised and sold a Space Passport, a kind of interplanetary driver's license, door to door. He was always so excited by space he thought it would be great if people one day had the chance to be interplanetary travelers. It was a "fun" item and he sold quite a few for $10 apiece in 1977.

One day he saw a small ad in the paper placed by a wealthy man wanting to buy meteorites, and realized they

Robert Haag, aka Meteorite Man, proudly displaying treasure from the heavens.

were worth something. Haag took a quick course on meteorites and then began running ads asking for them. He was twenty-three at the time. His first response came from a local man who had paid $10 for the small meteorite he owned. Haag bought it for $500. The first time he put it on display, he was offered $2,000.

He then began selling meteorites by mail and eventually had 3,500 clients worldwide. Many paid $200 for their chosen chunks from the sky, but hundreds spent more than $10,000. Then there were the serious collectors, who think nothing of spending $50,000 or more for a meteorite. What kept Haag going in the early days of his business was selling meteorites to the person whose ad he had seen originally. He was a member of the Du Pont family who died in 1990.

Haag has a vault under his Tucson house where he keeps his enormous collection of meteorites, which range in weight from half a gram to half a ton. The environment is climate-controlled, and he enters through the same type of massive door you would see in a bank vault. The walls inside are black, and the smaller meteorites are displayed on shelves while the heavy ones are on the floor.

Even Meteorite Man has a favorite, a treasure he must have. Just as those undersea treasure hunters had their hearts set on just one ship, as with Mel Fisher and the *Atocha,* Robert Haag's heart's desire is a piece of the Tucson meteor. He said that fragments from it are worth ten times the price of gold, but it isn't the monetary value that interests him, it's the idea of owning and touching a part of something so dynamic. The Tucson meteor is rare because there are so few pieces of it.

Early in the eighteenth century an unusually large meteor exploded before it hit the earth, as is usually the case. Spanish settlers found two large fragments south of Tucson and appropriately they came to be known as the Tucson meteorites. They were the earliest meteorites acquired by the Smithsonian Institution.

Haag has been diligently looking for fragments, which are practically in his own backyard. The canyon in which he has spent several years searching is not far from his home. He has 2,000 acres to cover in the area where, according to early accounts, those first large meteorites were found.

Haag said, "It's usually a nice day, it's fun and we like going out here and searching. It's treasure hunting."

He often uses a ParaPlane, which is similar to an ultralight but with a gas engine. It has also been described as a gas-propelled parachute. Haag said, "Any time a large meteorite comes in it makes a crater, a depression, and I'm looking for these low areas where sand and water collect. I use the ParaPlane because you can only see these craters when you're above the ground." When he finds a likely spot, he lands and uses a metal detector, which he describes as his meteorite finder. He said that he has found tons of them with it. He adds that the desert is an ideal landscape because the ground is exposed and it's easier to see meteorites.

Whenever Haag thinks he has found a meteorite, he takes it home and puts it in a weak acid solution to bring out the pattern inside. The patterns vary with the type of meteorite. Some have series of lines going both horizontally and vertically, and others have circles. For it to be a meteorite and not just a chunk of metal from some other source, it must exhibit the pattern when cut open. Some, such as the pallasite, which has circles inside, are quite beautiful. Haag has turned various meteorites into jewelry, watches, guitar picks, and even Buddhist knives.

This enterprise and Haag's business of marketing meteorites have not pleased a number of museum curators, who blame him for making collectibles out of scientific materials. They also feel it drives the price up, making it difficult for museums to compete with collectors.

In an interview in *The Wall Street Journal* in 1994, Haag responded to a quote from a curator who said that Haag wasn't a scientist but a dealer, and curators wished dealers would go away. Haag said, "It's not like that at all. Anyone can be a scientist and participate. And just think, you couldn't buy a star before, but now you can."

William Boynton, professor of planetary science at the University of Arizona in Tucson, spoke up for Haag, saying, "Robert finds things no one else will find."

Meanwhile, the delightful and optimistic Haag enjoys his life with his wife and two young daughters, continues making meteorites available to the world, and plans to keep searching for his elusive treasure. "No pieces yet of the Tucson meteorite," he said, "but maybe tomorrow." He added, "Meteorites are the coolest new collectible thing of all."

If you see a meteorite fall from the sky, you'll know who to call.

CHAPTER 27

GEMS OF PALA

Treasure hunting is far from scientific. This has never been made clearer than when a psychic found a treasure by sitting in a room far from the site and swinging a pendulum over a map.

During an interview with Ron Warmoth, who had an excellent reputation as a psychic and dowser, it was suggested he use his skill to discover if there were any valuable gems in southern California. His abilities had been documented in many newspaper articles and magazines, including a full page in *Newsweek.* Warmoth had clients in many parts of the world and was called upon to find locations for oil, precious gems, and gold. In addition, he had a good record of accurate information on the fluctuations of the stock market.

There was information that years ago working mines were producing rubies and garnets near Julian, California, not far from San Diego. However, no one, including Warmoth, knew if any of these mines were still operating.

It was a bright afternoon in December 1994 when Warmoth sat at the dining room table in a house on a winding street in the Hollywood Hills. There was a metal pendulum at the end of the chain he held over an official state map of a southern California area near San Diego. One of the locations on the map was the small town of Julian.

As Warmoth went over the entire map with his pendulum, there would be no response over some areas, while at others the pendulum would swiftly move in a small circle. Warmoth determined that the area some distance to the northwest of Julian would be the best place to search for and find treasure because of the strong signal from the pendulum.

Warmoth used a pendulum on maps and dowsing rods out in the field. To explain his methods he said, "The pendulum itself has no particular power or sort of energy of its own. All it's doing is reflecting what's coming from within myself, what's in the subconscious mind. You use these abilities as an extra sense, and that's what it means, extrasensory, but you use all known facts and then based upon it you make a conclusion. The only way you can test our work is to go out in the field and use it and then go by the evidence."

Information was obtained from the U.S. Forest Service that the Stewart tourmaline mine, also known as Gems of Pala, was a working mine in the area Warmoth had picked on the map. It was a private mine, but on weekends the public could visit and purchase buckets of rocks that had come from the mine and hope to find tourmalines. Many people did find them.

The next day Warmoth went to the Stewart mine, about 60 miles northwest of Julian. The hope was to find treasure and prove that his psychic dowsing predictions were accurate.

Blue Sheppard, left, owner of the Stewart tourmaline mine, also known as the Gems of Pala.

Blue Sheppard, the owner of the mine, was skeptical, and with good reason. He had never met Warmoth before. He had been mining since 1967 and explained that he had seen many dowsers and others making all sorts of claims as to their psychic abilities. However, once he and Warmoth sat down at a table on the porch of the Gems of Pala office, and Warmoth spread out a map of the mine that Sheppard provided, Sheppard became interested. "When Ron started showing me 'hot spots' on the map it got my attention," he said.

As Warmoth worked over the map with his pendulum he said, "I'm looking for the exceptional, for outstanding digs." He pointed out an area and Sheppard enthusiastically said, "Oh that's good." Warmoth added that he was looking for the pockets of pink tourmaline.

"They are the little nectars of the Stewart mine," Sheppard said. "This is what makes it so famous and considered by many experts to be the finest natural pink tourmaline in the world. It has a hot wild cherry color to it and when it's cut properly it's absolutely second to none."

He also pointed out that these tourmalines have been mined for over a hundred thirty-five years in San Diego County. In the early part of this century the Empress of China wanted tourmalines from the mine. The faceted stones sell for $1,000 a carat and up. Gem quality pink tourmalines are five times as rare as diamonds and, gram for gram, ten times as expensive as gold.

Before going into the mine to check out the area Warmoth suggested, Sheppard asked him to explain more about how the pendulum worked for him. Warmoth said, "As I work, primarily it's all mental, so it comes like a memory, as though I've seen it before and now I'm remembering it."

Sheppard said that he had heard other psychics say that the ability came from electromagnetic fields and gravity waves. Warmoth answered quickly and strongly, "Nonsense, nonsense." He then continued to use his pendulum over the map of the mine and to give his opinion on where a new pocket of tourmaline would be found. "My impression is that you go into these green zones and these bluish zones that the pendulum is indicating on the map." He was referring to the coloring in the rock inside the mine but had no way of knowing that the areas he noted had green or blue at those spots.

"Man, how do you know all this?" Sheppard asked, and noted that the problem in this type of mining is that the pockets of tourmaline are very small and the mine very large, so it is like looking for a needle in a haystack. Sheppard said it is often easier to find other types of gems and gold than it is to find the tourmalines.

As they entered the mine Sheppard said, "When I come under the ground I feel a charge of energy. I feel the excitement, a lot of invigoration and a lot of inspiration. That's a disease. To find and discover and touch something that's never been touched before. I'm like a kid and this is my candy store."

Sheppard and Warmoth went into the mine, and Warmoth was able to find three areas he had chosen on the map. Sheppard said, "When Ron was on the porch, dowsing the map, he picked several areas that would be good. Once we went into the mine, he was able to go to them without my help. It's a big mine and he had never been there before, and he would not have been able to memorize the location from looking at the map." At the first two locations Warmoth said that the tourmalines were about 30 feet inside the rock. This would have necessitated blasting, so he continued to an area 60 by 80 feet, which is one of the sections he had pinpointed on the map. Then Warmoth said that in this location the tourmaline was close to the surface. He pointed to a specific spot, and Sheppard began chipping away there with his pick. Sheppard said, "Look how this pocket is opening up. There really wasn't any strong indicator until Ron dowsed the map about ten minutes ago and now here's a pocket of tourmaline."

After Sheppard worked on the rock for just a few more minutes, he was able to hold a gem in his hand. "Here's a pink tourmaline in its first second of arrival into the world of light. I can see it's going to cut into a small, faceted gemstone which will have quite a bit of value for its size. We'll keep looking for the big one." Sheppard later said that the value of the tourmaline after cutting was about $4,000.

As they continued, Sheppard talked about mining, something he loves because he is a true treasure hunter. "There's a lot of struggle in mining, so when somebody finds something really fantastic, you're reminded to ask, 'How many years did this guy struggle?' "

As the day ended, Sheppard had treasure and Warmoth had validation of his ability. "He really came in and pointed on the map and then later to the same place underground where tourmaline just shouldn't have been," Sheppard said. "He said it was there and it was. That's proof for me."

A short time later Sheppard worked on one of the other areas Warmoth had picked on the map and then found inside the mine. He said, "This was the location where Ron said the tourmaline was about 30 feet inside the rock. Before I met him, I had marked this area as a possibility. Ron, of course, did not know this when he dowsed the map. We blasted at the location and opened up a large pocket of tourmaline. The total value when we had finished was close to $200,000."

Needless to say, many people were impressed by Warmoth's work, and he was contacted by those who wanted his help in finding quite a variety of treasure.

In December 1998, Ron Warmoth died. This was unexpected by many of those who knew and admired him. He was an exceptional person, one of the most knowledgeable on a wide variety of subjects, and a true gentleman. He will be missed by all those whose lives he touched.

CHAPTER 28

The Diving Couple

Bob and Margaret Weller may look like the couple next door, but that's where the similarity ends, because one's neighbors probably haven't found millions of dollars' worth of treasure. The Wellers have. What started as a hobby became a lucrative business.

After twenty-five years of marriage and diving together, they have achieved status as two of the most successful treasure hunters in the world. This could be because they live in Florida and are in close proximity to the many wrecks up and down the coast where the treasure laden galleons bound for Spain met an untimely end.

Margaret was raised in Jamaica, which gave her an early love of the sea. She says, "When you find something, even if it's the first time you're out and you find some pottery shards, it's a thrill. You know you've found a piece of the wreck. Sometimes it's years before you find that first piece of gold

Bob and Margaret Weller, © Allen Eyestone/*The Palm Beach Post*

Bob and Margaret Weller, displaying one of their finds.

and when you do, you'll never forget that feeling. When I found my first piece of gold, I couldn't stop giggling. It went on for a week and people would look at me and I'd burst out laughing for no reason. You just have this tremendous high, this enthusiasm."

That enthusiasm has never waned and the Wellers have been subcontracting for Mel Fisher on the 1715 fleet for some time. They have found Spanish gold and silver coins, gold rings, and a fantastic 11-foot-long gold chain that alone is worth $60,000, as well as many other valuable artifacts. It seems that the Spanish had a penchant for putting gold into chains of varying lengths, but mainly quite long chains.

Margaret says that each artifact is a piece of history and tells a story that is very important to them. "We found a gold bar, for example, that tells the story of a wealthy Colombian family that had its own mint. There were tax stamps on it." Those markings were etched into the gold.

Bob is also a prolific writer and researcher and has written a number of books on treasure and treasure hunters. The various markings on the gold and other artifacts add to his continued bank of information on Spain and the New World from the time of Columbus to the 1800s.

"You have to have patience to keep going day after day when you find nothing," he says. "You're fighting the elements, poor weather, and zero visibility. Just when you're about to give up things change. Once you begin to find treasure, it all becomes worthwhile."

The Wellers don't limit their diving to the 1715 fleet, and have been to various wrecks including the ships of the 1733 fleet off Key Largo, Florida.

Margaret is particularly fascinated by the collection of gold and jeweled rings she has retrieved from the ocean floor. "What stories the rings could tell," she says, and adds, "There are days when you're about to say 'I've had enough of this' and the ocean gives you back something. You pick up a gold coin and say, 'Oh my, look at this!'"

One of their favorite treasures is an ornate gold and amethyst ring that was found on the *Nieves,* a wreck from the 1715 fleet off Fort Pierce. It is significant to Margaret because "This has lain on the bottom of the ocean for over 300 years and it's in perfect condition."

The Wellers hearken back to another diving couple, Mel and Deo Fisher, who began their road to treasure-hunting expertise and fame diving on the wrecks of the 1715 fleet.

Bob was a frogman in the navy and began diving for treasure in 1960. He says, "My first wreck, the one I cut my teeth on, was *El Infante* of the 1733 fleet off Key Largo." He did extensive research and learned the details of what happened after the fleet sailed into the path of a hurricane.

On July 13, 1733, the annual Spanish treasure fleet left Havana Harbor, twenty ships heading home. The lead ship was always known as the "Capitana." In this fleet it was *El Rui* and was a war galleon with sixty cannons. On the right flank was *El Enfante,* another war galleon with sixty cannons. By the evening of the second day the winds were rising and the seas mounting and by morning the Capitana was heading back to Havana Harbor with the others following. What the fleet commander didn't know was that a hurricane was passing over Cuba and they were directly in its path. By the time the hurricane had passed, July 16, *El Enfante* had come to rest against a reef and the crew could see the coast and the beginning of Key Largo. The other ships were grounded in various locations. Miraculously, the crew and passengers reached land safely by using the patched ship's launch, a small boat used to take people to and from shore, and a large raft built from parts of the ship.

The Spanish, accustomed to shipwrecks, tried to salvage the treasures quickly, if possible, and in this case the work began August 7. By September 9, 180 boxes of silver coin had been recovered, only one box short of the registered treasure.

It wasn't until the late 1950s, more than 220 years later, that commercial salvage of *El Enfante* began. A single gold coin was found, a number of silver coins, swords, pistols, and a variety of other items.

When Bob Weller was attempting his first salvage work on *El Enfante* in 1960, he says that underwater metal detectors would have been heaven-sent, but in those days it was visual recovery. He found three gold rings, a gold medallion, buttons, buckles, hundreds of silver coins, cannonballs, and piles of musket balls. One of the gold rings became Margaret's wedding ring when they married.

Salvage work continues to this day. It is on a small scale because the Spanish actually brought up most of the treasure right after the ship went down. Weller says that scuba divers occasionally recover a coin or two and a little gold. It is the most visited wreck in the Florida Keys. The hull lies buried under sand, but the water is crystal clear and 16 feet deep. He says, "It's a great escape from telephones and traffic!"

The Wellers have conducted classes for diving enthusiasts who want the thrill of treasure hunting. Small groups stay at their home and use the 1715 fleet as a training ground.

Their ongoing enthusiasm is boundless. Bob is now planning to be the first to salvage the *San Jose* off Cartagena, Colombia, the ship described as the richest Spanish treasure vessel in the world. Her whereabouts has eluded many, but Bob says he knows the location.

The Wellers' commitment to each other and treasure hunting shows that, in their case, the couple that swims together stays together!

CHAPTER 29

The Storage Locker Treasure

It's one thing to search for treasure and not find it; but it's another, more heartbreaking, experience to be near a fortune and not know it.

For eight years, Mike Prindiville had managed storage facilities in Los Angeles, California, where it was not unusual for people to abandon their belongings. "Someone had paid a long time in advance for a room, but then he didn't pay for about a year and we couldn't find him," Mike said.

Whenever this happened the procedure was to cut off the locks and hold auctions on the items inside, because the company wanted to rent the space again. However, when Prindiville and the others went into the room, it was empty except for a lone blue trunk.

"People want rooms of furniture, not a trunk, so we put it in the vault and saw it and passed it every day," Prindiville

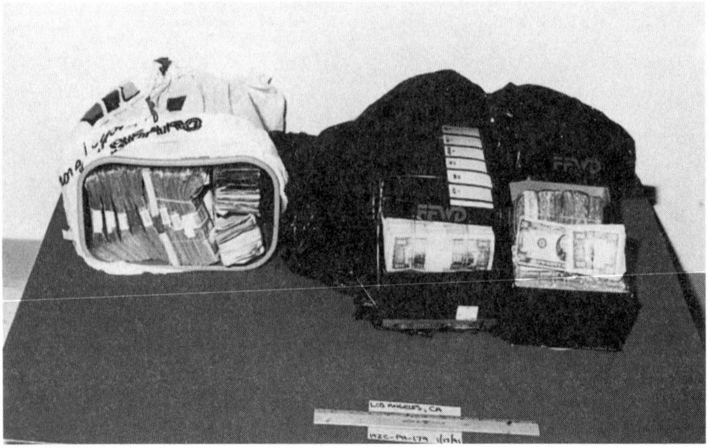

Money recovered by the FBI from a storage locker in Los Angeles.

said. "It was locked so we never tried to open it. We thought the owner might come back sometime and claim it."

It was a typical day at the facility in January 1991 when, suddenly, FBI agents arrived with a search warrant for the trunk. After recovering from their surprise, Prindiville and the others realized the trunk they wanted must be the one in the vault, and they brought it out. When the trunk was opened, there were stacks of cash inside. Some of the money was in shoe boxes. It took time to count it and determine the total, but from first glance, FBI agents knew there would be hundreds of thousands of dollars.

It all began when Edward Leigh Hunt, Jr., a man who had no previous criminal record, robbed a security truck in Philadelphia in 1988 and managed to get away with $651,000. He was 24 and had been working for the company for several months. Some time later, authorities in Hunt's hometown of Wilmington, Delaware, contacted the FBI office in Philadelphia stating that they had received a call from Hunt, who said he had committed the crime. He wanted to turn himself in at the front of the Los Angeles Chamber of Commerce building on January 20, 1990, the second anniversary of the robbery.

FBI agent Ralph Di Fonzo said, "The case first came to me when I was assigned to the major case squad in Los Angeles and I arrested him." Hunt said he had gambled all the money away by using a scheme that obviously didn't work. He said he had planned to repay what he had stolen by gambling.

Hunt's father, a prominent attorney in Wilmington, and his mother, a teacher, had not heard from their son in the two years before his arrest in Los Angeles. Hunt was a 1985 graduate in psychology from the University of Delaware, where he was on the dean's list. After college he worked in several odd jobs until he was hired by the security company. According to interviews with his parents, he had never been arrested for anything, had never even received a traffic ticket. On the day of the robbery, Hunt was left in the truck while two other guards went inside a bank. When they returned, Hunt and two bags of cash were gone. The family had no idea why he committed the crime.

Even though none of the money from the robbery was ever found, Hunt was convicted and sentenced to eight years in federal prison, always insisting that he had lost everything gambling. About a year into his sentence he decided to reveal the whereabouts of the money.

Because he was in charge of bringing in the trunk, Di Fonzo was once again involved with the man he had arrested. He gave his opinion of why Hunt decided to divulge the whereabouts of the money. "He was no hardened criminal, and when you get that type in prison they will sometimes do anything to make a deal to reduce the sentence.

"We couldn't believe the amount of money in the trunk until we counted it," Di Fonzo said. "I had to count it three times. It took a long time to count $575,000. It probably took longer to count it than to arrest the subject, take him to jail, and book him." He added, "I know no one knew that money was there or it probably wouldn't have been there that long."

"If we had auctioned the trunk, it would have gone to the highest bidder, for maybe $5," Prindiville said. "We're not required to keep records so the person would have kept it."

Since the FBI had a search warrant there was no reward for Prindiville. All he could say was, "$575,000 in cash sitting under my nose all this time!"

Perhaps the moral of this tale is that if you find a mysterious trunk is up for sale and it's cheap . . . buy it!

CHAPTER 30

The Oldest Levi's

People who enjoy looking for treasure often go to the abandoned mining towns, or ghost towns, that are found throughout Nevada and Arizona. The hope is to find gold, but one man's discovery showed that there are other treasures lurking in unexpected places.

After gold was discovered in California in 1848, throngs of people from this and other countries rushed to the site to make their fortunes. They needed sturdy work clothes so they could pursue the hard and dirty job of finding gold. Some of these men were city folk who had never worked outdoors and did not have appropriate clothing. A Bavarian immigrant named Levi Strauss happened to be in the right place at the right time to fill the need. He was a dry goods merchant in San Francisco and there, Levi's were born.

Levi's became popular quickly and, along with the mining tools, became a necessary part of the equipment. Some lucky miners made a fortune while wearing Levi's, and Strauss started an empire. Levi's became a symbol of the United States and by the 1950s, a fashion statement. Other jeans have come and gone, but Levi's reign eternal.

One hundred and fifty years after Levi Strauss made the first jeans, a young truck driver was poking around in a ghost town in central Nevada. He was near the opening of a small abandoned mine when he saw a shack nearby. When he entered the shack, he saw some broken tools and a boxful of old, ratty clothing that was so dirty, he really didn't want to touch it. However, he knew of Ron Hamilton of Cookeville, Tennessee, who is a leading supplier of vintage clothing for people who take part in historical reenactments, especially Civil War battles. The truck driver thought he would send the box of clothing to Hamilton, who was always on the lookout for something old and unusual.

When Hamilton received the box, he was appalled at the filthy clothes and rocks inside. He dumped out the contents and saw some shirts, a coat, shoes, and a pair of pants. "I was about to get rid of all of it because it was so 'nasty,' but at the last moment I decided I would wash the pants," Hamilton said. After five cycles in the washing machine, he recognized the pants as Levi's, possibly the oldest pair he had ever seen. He knew that in 1996 Levi Strauss and Company had paid $25,000 for a pair estimated to be a hundred years old, believed to be the oldest pair at that time. The sale made newspaper headlines around the country.

Hamilton called Levi Strauss to discuss his find. He said that the woman who answered told him that it seemed everyone was calling to report they had a pair of the oldest Levi's. He said that she asked him, "Have you washed them?" When

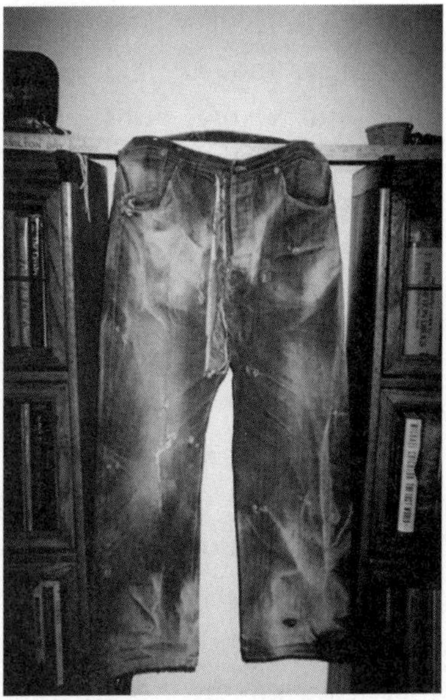

A pair of Levi's which date back to the beginning of the 20th century.

he said that he had, she said, "Oh, no!" When he told her it took five washings to get the mud out, she asked, "Did they stay together?" Hamilton said, "Sure, they're Levi's." The woman had him describe them. He said that there was one back pocket, and she replied, "That's 1906. After that there were two back pockets." He told her that the inner pockets were the same fabric as the outer pockets and she said, "That makes them 1900 to 1902." When Hamilton said the jeans had a side pocket similar to a pliers pocket on work pants, the woman said that they were not Levi's.

Hamilton told her it said *Levi Strauss* on the rivets, so he was asked to send a picture of his "find." The problem was that in the 1906 San Francisco earthquake and the fire that followed, the Levi Strauss building was one of the many totally destroyed. They have no records of their famous jeans before 1906. After the pictures of Hamilton's Levi's arrived, he was told the company couldn't say for sure that they were the oldest pair. He said he was offered $30,000, but he didn't want to sell because he was determined to know if he really had the oldest pair. Hamilton said the woman he first contacted is no longer with the company.

Hamilton looked for an independent expert to help him verify the age of the Levi's. He found Zip Stevenson, a denim collector and restorer in the Los Angeles area. Stevenson buys, sells, and wears vintage Levi's. He often can be seen wearing a pair worth $2,500. As others search for gold, Stevenson searches for that extraordinary pair of jeans that will be the "big score," a pair that will be worth several thousand dollars or more. He is a regular at the Rose Bowl swap meets in Pasadena, where people from around the world who are crazy for Levi's come to buy. Japanese tourists particularly want Levi's and flock to Stevenson's area, where they pay $500 for 501's from 1967, and $2,500 for double xx's (501xx) from the 1950s.

Hamilton brought his Levi's to Stevenson, who said, "Man, these are amazing. The coin pocket way up on the waistband and the primitive stitching is so amazing. The tool or ruler pocket is so unique. I've never even heard people talking about this existing. This jean is like 120 years old. Yep, this is the oldest pair of Levi's. I'm confident about it. It's a 'killer' pair. Whatever the top of the market is, whether it's $10,000 or a million, your pair is it. It's a special piece and you really have a treasure, congratulations."

Hamilton was delighted to have his Levi's verified and certainly considers them a treasure. He believes they are the oldest pair and is proud to hold on to a symbol of this country's past. He said, "It's history, it's America, it's who we are. The cowboy history is the only history that we have in the United States and that's different from the rest of the world's."

This story shows that you not only need an eagle eye to spot something of value, but you need to know where to show it after you've found it. Remember, one person's junk is another person's treasure.

CHAPTER 31

The Lost Race Cars

You would think that record-holding race cars would be well cared for, even after retirement, but, unfortunately, many disappear or end up in junkyards. Here is the story of a man with a mission who found and restored some of these automotive treasures.

Bruce Meyer, a Los Angeles businessman and car collector said, "I've been a car buff since birth. I think you're born with those genes, but as a serious collector, I bought my first car after college in the early 60s. I've been trading up ever since." Meyer was particularly drawn to race cars and owns the Agajanian Special, which won the Indianapolis race in 1952. It was driven by Troy Ruttman, who at twenty-two was the youngest driver ever to win the race. Meyer also owns a Duesenberg, a large luxury car of the 1920s and 1930s, but the race cars are really his favorites. One in particular was important to him. It was the So-Cal Belly Tank, a dry lakes racer that set many records in the early 1950s but had stopped running by 1953, when the type of engine used in those cars changed. Meyer said, "This car meant a great deal to me when I was growing up because of the beautiful graphics and how it was put together. It was an icon for dry lake racing and had the Bonneville world record of 198 miles per hour. It was a car everyone knew." The So-Cal Belly Tank had been on the cover of *Hot Rod* magazine more than once. Meyer said, "The car was missing for years and all the hot-rodders and dry lakes fellas were looking for it." Whenever Meyer was with "car people" he would ask about the So-Cal Belly Tank, but no one seemed to know where it was.

Bonneville refers to the salt flats in Utah where many drivers brought their cars, hoping to set a record and become part of racing history. A record at Bonneville for dry lake racers would be like winning the Indianapolis 500-mile race in the powerful championship race cars that run on long-distance tracks. Bonneville racing was a difficult task because, to set the record, the car and driver had to make a return run, before which, because of the high speed, they would have to stop the car completely. The two runs were made because an average was taken of the time. Wind played a factor, and when the car was running with the wind the time would be faster than when going against it. Many times the cars had mechanical problems on that second stage. Drivers, car owners, and mechanics often left Utah with shattered dreams. Some returned year after year but never did set the record.

The So-Cal Belly Tank was made from one of the two drop-fuel tanks of a P-38 fighter from World War II. Alex Xydias, a car builder, said, "After the war there were surplus

The So-Cal Belly Tank, a record-setting dry lakes racer from the 1950s.

stores in Los Angeles that had these surplus belly tanks that were under the fuselage of the plane and not out near the wing, where they were in other planes. It was perfect to use." The fuel tank had an oval, bulletlike appearance, and the entire body of the car was the tank.

In southern California, where speed was king in the fifties, racing was a way of life. Two dry lakes, El Mirage and Muroc, were used for racing. Both were within a hundred-mile radius of Los Angeles, and there the cars ran, hoping to set a record and go on to glory at Bonneville.

In 1994, Meyer was having dinner with Xydias at a reunion of hot-rodders in Bakersfield, California. Meyer said, "Alex heard that the So-Cal Belly Tank was in a barn, in a loft with some relics near Los Angeles. Immediately, my treasure light went off. I had to find it."

Meyer could barely wait to get to that barn and find the

car. On March 19, 1994, he and Xydias went to the barn in Redondo Beach, California. What they entered was a cavernous, Quonset hut–type barn, and after searching, saw the shell of the once sleek So-Cal Belly Tank way up in the rafters. When Xydias saw it he thought it was almost worthless. He said, "It showed decades of neglect." In contrast, Meyer was ecstatic. "I thought it was wonderful because all the parts were there. I knew it could be restored." After they began taking the car down, bit by bit, Xydias said, "It was like digging up buried treasure when we dug it out of the rafters."

Meyer had the car completely restored and it is now proudly displayed in the Peterson Automotive Museum in Los Angeles. Dick Messer, director of the museum, said that the car is a real treasure since it is one of a kind. It's difficult to put an actual value on it but it is certainly worth a great deal and the value will increase in the future. Meyer says he has no plans to sell it. "Would I take $250,000 for it? No. Is it worth $50,000? Who knows? I'm just glad I have this treasure."

In Meyer's ongoing quest to find race cars, he heard about another famous one and was responsible for restoring it. It was the Greer-Black-Prudhomme dragster, and even though it helped put drag-racing on the map in the 1960s, it disappeared once its glory days were over. The car was named for its builders and driver. Tom Greer was a machine shop owner, Keith Black an engine builder, and Don (the Snake) Prudhomme, the legendary and daring driver who won 236 races out of 243. Meyer said that it was a record that will never be broken. The car roared down the quarter-mile drag strips around southern California and left spectators in awe. At speeds nearing 200 miles an hour, it took a parachute release to make it stop. Eventually, cars became faster and bigger and the Greer-Black-Prudhomme car was left in the dust. Unbelievably, the car was dismantled and parts and pieces were used in other cars.

In the 1980s, Steve Davis, a race car builder, began searching for the car. It was a long, slow ordeal. He found that it had once been sold to a junkyard in Nevada for about $4,000, then resold several times. Davis finally found the car in a desolate boneyard outside Reno, Nevada. There was no motor or drive train, and the front axle was broken in half. Davis paid $1,000 for the wreck and was thrilled to have it. Then he set out on the seemingly impossible task of finding all the original parts. He became a super-sleuth, checking sales receipts from junkyards and talking with auto parts people. He found almost every part, and what he couldn't find he had made to exact specifications. However, he needed help financially in order to restore the treasure. Bruce Meyer stepped in, bought the car, then hired Davis to do the complete restoration. It is now back to its former glory and can be seen in the National Hot Rod Association Museum in Pomona, California. The car has also toured the country, allowing new generations of car enthusiasts to see one of the "greats."

Meyer said that car experts have put a value of half a million dollars on the car, but he has no plans to sell. These cars are his treasures and are a link to those glory days of racing that he will always remember.

If you pass a junkyard full of old cars, keep your eyes open for one resembling a race car. It could turn out to be your treasure because collectors are ready and waiting.

CHAPTER 32

The Lost Squadron

Some people dig in the ground for gold or jewels, while others dive under the sea to search for riches. This is the tale of a man who drilled 268 feet into the ice to find his treasure.

J. Roy Shoffner, a teenager in Middlesboro, Kentucky, during World War II, dreamed of flying the P-38 Lightning for the Army Air Corps. He was too young at the time to fly the fastest plane in the sky. Ten thousand of these fighter bombers that flew at 400 miles per hour were built at Lockheed Aircraft in Burbank, California, beginning in 1942. It was their twin supercharged engines that gave them top speed. They were feared by the enemy and revered by American pilots.

"The P-38 was the best airplane we had at the time," Shoffner said. He added that it was the only one that had five automatic weapons on it: four 50-caliber machine guns, and one 20-millimeter cannon.

After the war the government disposed of 250,000 planes, and the P-38 became one of the rarest because hardly any of them were left. Shoffner continued to think about the plane as years went by. Even after he became a pilot during the Korean War, his dream never wavered. He wanted to fly a P-38.

A chain of events beginning in World War II would one day bring Shoffner to his dream plane. On July 4, 1942, eight P-38s and two B-17s left Presque-Isle, Maine, and headed across the North Atlantic for delivery in England. The trip was made in stages. The first stop was Goose Bay, Labrador, then Greenland, Iceland, and finally England. Brad McManus, one of the pilots, provided details. "At the midway point, the message came back that Reykjavik, Iceland, was closed, so at that point we turned back and headed for the base from which we had departed. Foul weather had closed Greenland as well as Iceland and it was time for decisive action. I decided then and there, I'm going in while I still have control of my airplane. I dropped out of the flight plan and went down and made a pass over the ice cap. It looked smooth and clear so I dropped my gear and set the airplane down in Greenland."

Amazingly, the entire squadron survived the landing on the ice cap. The men waited there for ten days until they were rescued. McManus said, "The war was so busy on all fronts, I'm sure no one thought twice about trying to rescue those planes." They were occasionally seen by planes flying over, and finally disappeared under the snow after severe storms.

The legend of the Lost Squadron, as it came to be known, spread far and wide. Many aviation-loving treasure hunters tried to find the invisible planes, but even after some thought they had the spot, all attempts to retrieve the planes failed. After fifty years of harsh winters, they were under 268 feet of ice.

News of the Lost Squadron reached Shoffner in Middlesboro and brought back his fervent wish to own and fly a P-38. After his military service, he prospered and in the 1980s began collecting and restoring planes. They were a J-3 Piper Cub 1945, which was destroyed in a tornado; a J-5 Piper Cub that was totally in need of repairs; a 1930 Waco Bi-Plane Aero-Basic open cockpit; and a 1931 Waco Bi-Plane that had been hanging in a barn for thirty-five years. The four planes are now in flying condition.

Shoffner owned the local Kentucky Fried Chicken and the Dairy Queen, as well as the supermarket and local bank. "It's always been my forte to do something that no one else has done before," Shoffner said. "I did that in all my business and it's brought me gratification. To bore down to 268 feet and take an aircraft apart and bring it to the surface, and then restore it to flying condition, has never been done."

He launched the thirteenth attempt to recover one of the planes with the necessary ingredients for success. He had money, the passion of wanting to fly a P-38, and the know-how to achieve his goal. A group was assembled, and on May 6, 1992, the work began. It was an almost overwhelming undertaking, fraught with many obstacles. The crew had to have food and housing and protection from the extreme cold. In addition, they had to have a supply route as well as a plan to remove the plane from 268 feet of ice. No matter what he faced, Shoffner was determined to succeed.

Bob Cardin, the project manager, described the procedure. "We used radar to find the plane. Then we made a six-inch-in-diameter probe hole and put a probe down to be sure we had the plane. Next we melted a four-foot-diameter shaft down to the plane. A closed system hot water drill we called the 'gopher' pumped 180-degree hot water down. The water would sit on the ice, and the ice would melt, and gravity would pull it down. At the rate of two feet per hour, it took the 'gopher' a week to get down to the plane." Shoffner worried that if the ice surrounding the shaft cracked, it would fill with water and the men would have a terrible time getting up and out. The first day they went down the hole it cracked and popped, but held.

They wondered what shape the plane would be in as they pumped hot water down. Finally, the plane took shape as though out of an ice cube. They couldn't imagine how they could get it out, but they did, piece by piece. They brought up pieces of the wing and the entire 2,000-pound engine, as well as smaller pieces. The last piece to come up was the 7,000-pound center section. It took two full days to take it out of the hole—another major accomplishment.

There was a great deal of hard work ahead for the determined group. The pieces had to go by helicopter, ship, and truck to the hangar in Middlesboro. When the plane arrived, Shoffner realized that the crushing weight of the ice had left it in worse condition than they had thought. Every piece was broken, so they began fixing it, a piece at a time. The plane, which they had named *Glacier Girl,* was slowly being brought back to life, fifty-five years after she disappeared. The P-38 was one of only a few remaining in the world.

Shoffner and the others wanted the reconstruction to be 100 percent authentic. Eighty percent of the original plane

The remains of a P-38 from the Lost Squadron, unearthed from its tomb in Greenland.

has been saved, and the remaining pieces are being remanufactured from the original parts. They were able to save some of the air from those 1942 tires and put it back in the new tires.

Shoffner said, "This is one of the most valuable aircraft restorations in existence in the world today. The value can't be less than eight million dollars when completed. We're going to have a plane that anyone would want. It's been a three-part story. First the elation of going after it. Then bringing it out and building it back to flying condition, and then the elation of flying it home."

After over five years of work, he estimates another two years to complete the labor of love. Then he plans to fly his dream machine around the country so everyone can see it.

"It's a wonderful piece of our heritage and deserves to be shown," Shoffner said.

All those still alive who flew the P-38, and the others who dreamed of doing so, will agree that Shoffner has truly found an amazing treasure.

CHAPTER 33

Civil War Uniform

A collector spent twenty-five years looking for a relic of the Civil War and found it with items from World Wars I and II. No one has any idea of how it got there.

There has always been something about the Civil War that has captivated people ever since that tragic conflict. As years pass the mystique grows, and among others who devote nearly all their time studying the events, there are now a number of groups that yearly stage reenactments of the major battles. Probably more amateur historians are researching every aspect of this war than any other fought by our country. Photography was in its infancy at the time, so there are few pictures of the terrible events. For this reason, the historical artist has been a bridge to the past, the one who gives life to the battles and lets people see the great bloodshed, death, and destruction. Don Troiani of Southbury, Connecticut, devotes his life and art to providing a glimpse into the war that pitted brother against brother in some cases, and friend against friend. It takes meticulous research and attention to detail to accomplish his task.

Troiani said, "I'm a collector, a researcher, a student of uniforms and equipage, and a painter. All these specialties combine into one to turn out a very precise kind of painting. I have to know if they were charging through rye, or clover, or wheat. If it had rained the day before. Would their feet be muddy or dusty? I have to also understand how the clothes were tailored because Civil War clothing is cut completely differently than modern clothing. It hangs on the body differently, and the materials are different. It gives me an understanding that I can't get elsewhere." Troiani adds that he must know the type of uniform that was worn. This is very difficult because at the beginning of the war, volunteer regiments showed up in a variety of colors and styles.

Troiani goes to great lengths to get authenticity in his paintings, which has made him one of the top collectors of Civil War uniforms. The one that he has always wanted, and that he searches for diligently, is the most sought-after of Civil War uniforms: the Berdan sharpshooter uniform.

Mike McAfee, Curator of History at the West Point Museum, said, "The sharpshooter mystique is probably one of the reasons why the Berdan uniform is so sought after. Also, the fact that they just don't seem to exist. The uniforms that survive in quantities are the common uniforms that were left over after the war, actually as surplus. The uniforms used by the individual soldiers usually got used up, thrown away, or maybe the soldier was buried in it. So to find a uniform that wasn't available after the war as surplus, still surviving today, is quite rare."

"I've been looking for a Berdan sharpshooter uniform for the 25 years I've been collecting uniforms," Troiani said. "I don't know anyone who's found one. I know of none other than the one in the Smithsonian. To me, it would be the ultimate artifact for a Civil War uniform collector. I can't think of anything I would want more."

He explains that when the war began in 1861, everyone seemed to think it would be over quickly. The first enlistments were for ninety days, but by late summer it was evident that the war would not be over soon. In answer to the Union's call for recruits, regiments of volunteers formed up in all states. Colonel Hiram Berdan formed a regiment of sharpshooters, but had so many recruits that they formed two regiments. Each man had to be very proficient in arms and target shooting. To qualify for the regiment, each man had to pass a shooting test that consisted of hitting a 10-inch circle ten consecutive times from a distance of 200 yards. Berdan's men used Model 1859 Sharps breechloaders, which were the most rapid-fire and accurate weapons. Some men had special long-range target rifles that could hit a person at 700 yards. The other feature that made the unit stand out was the distinctive green uniform.

McAfee said, "Berdan talked about using green as a camouflage, green in summer, maybe gray in winter." He added that in the war they were first into battle, first to reconnoiter positions, and first in harm's way.

"They were well known from the beginning, and great things were expected of them," Troiani said. "They did deliver in the course of the war and they were pretty much visible on every battlefield. Everyone knew who they were, especially the Confederates. Berdan sharpshooters claimed

The coat from a uniform of one of the Berdan sharpshooters, one of the most feared regiments of marksmen in the Civil War.

to have killed or wounded more Confederates than any other regiment, but no one can be sure. It seems a good possibility. Their casualty rate was among the highest on the Union side." He added that they were one of the units used up during the war by disease and casualties. Because they were almost always engaged, they seemed to lose more men than other regiments. That is one reason the uniform is so rare.

For years Troiani dug through attics and went to auctions and rummage sales, hoping to find the uniform. Late in 1996 he was reading auction notices one day and saw that at a nearby auction there would be mostly clothing. His wife said, "Oh don't go," but he knew he had to be there. Other collectors often talked about the fact that things they really wanted turned up when they weren't there.

At the auction there were boxes of uniforms. Troiani always went through the entire box carefully, not just the pieces on top. In this case he first saw some World War II uniforms but couldn't assume that was it, that the whole box was only World War II. He kept going deeper into the box, and at the bottom there it was—a green Berdan sharpshooter uniform. He couldn't believe it. His heart began to beat faster and he broke out in a sweat. It had been twenty-five years of searching, and here it was in the bottom of the box. What stories that uniform could tell, and what tragedy had been part of the life of the sharpshooter. Just to touch it brought a flood of emotion.

Troiani covered it up quickly, hoping that no other collectors would show up. He had to sit quite a while, waiting for the box once the auction began. He waited for three hours because it was a numbered sale, and the box with the uniform was near the end. He said, "It was quite a sweat. Of course you wonder who's going to be bidding. Who else knows? It's hard to decide on a one-of-a-kind item what you're going to spend. It's something that might never come up again. I was prepared to go as high as $20,000, but once the bidding started, who knows? I might have gone higher. I was going to get it no matter what."

The bidding started at $25, and quickly went up to $300 as Troiani bid against the others. Then he went to $325, and the whole box of uniforms was his. An antique dealer asked him if he could buy the rest of the items in the box for $225, and Troiani sold them to him. He said, "So I got the uniform for $100. The bargain of a lifetime." He was thrilled to have his treasure in his hands. The uniform had the high-standing collar, green color, and special nonreflective Goodyear buttons that made the frock coat unique in the Union Army.

He had to check to be sure his find was authentic. During the war, the men often had their names in their uniforms. Troiani checked and there it was. The name of the sharpshooter, William Frank Tilson, written in the sleeve along with his company. With this information Troiani was able to do research, and learned that Tilson was with the Second U.S. Sharpshooters and served in 1862. He was wounded by a shell at Petersburg, where he lost his leg. It was amputated below the knee.

Being able to attach a name to the uniform increases the historical significance and the monetary one as well. McAfee said, "A surplus enlisted man's frock coat in good condition could be worth $10,000 to $15,000, so here's a one-of-a-kind coat worn by an individual soldier. It's hard to say what this one is actually worth."

Brendan M. Synnamon, co-owner of The Union Drummer Boy store in Gettysburg, Pennsylvania, and an expert on Civil War uniforms said, "The Berdan sharpshooter coat is one of a kind. It could easily be worth $30,000 to $50,000. I sold a nondescript major's hat from the Civil War for $20,000. It had braiding on it that showed the rank and that the man was a surgeon, but there was no name inside."

Troiani said, "I don't think I would take anything for it. I think if you offered me $100,000 I wouldn't take it, but realistically, I think it would be worth about $40,000. Now, of course, a lot of Civil War uniforms are not worth anything like that price. This is the rarest of them all. The pinnacle of Civil War collecting."

Troiani found his treasure and in doing so, honored the gallant soldier who wore the uniform.

CHAPTER 34

THE SALVADOR DALÍ PAINTING

In the world of treasure hunting, the first one at the scene often gets the prize. This was the case when a man who knew the value of timing found his treasure in the back of a thrift shop.

On a December day in 1994, Robert Loughlin made certain he was first in line at the door of a new Salvation Army thrift shop in SoHo, an area of New York City. It was the opening day, which Loughlin knew was the best time to find the special items that might bring him a profit. He was known to antique dealers and others in the field as a picker, someone who sells his finds to dealers and hopes for the special treasure worthy of being auctioned at the more prestigious companies.

Loughlin went swiftly to the back of the thrift shop and looked it over carefully. He saw a rolled-up canvas under a rack of men's clothes and quickly picked it up. When he

Dalí painting of Marquis de Cuevas.

opened the canvas he found a lovely portrait of a man in a surreal landscape. Upon closer inspection he saw that the painting was signed "Salvador Dalí, 1942." He wasn't sure, but he had a hunch the painting might be the real thing, so he decided to buy it before someone else did. The asking price was $50, but when he reached the cash register he was able to bargain the price down to $40.

Dalí was born near Barcelona, Spain, in 1904 and studied art in Madrid for several years. As a young man in his twenties he was briefly influenced by such abstract painters as Picasso and Miró, but soon went back to his early interest in metaphysical painting. In his 1942 autobiography, *The Secret Life of Salvador Dalí*, he said that he had many extraordinarily intense emotional experiences as a child in which many of his later dreams and obsessions were prefigured. When Dalí moved to Paris in 1929, he officially became a Surrealist painter, depicting on canvas the hallucinatory atmosphere of dreams. He also used objects in his painting, especially clocks. One that attracted a great deal of attention was "Persistence of Memory," a landscape with limp watches hanging over various objects in the picture.

Surrealism is a style of art that emphasizes fantasy; its subjects are usually the experiences revealed by the unconcious mind. The purpose of the movement is to show levels of consciousness not ordinarily associated with everyday life.

Dalí moved to the United States in 1940 and died in 1989. He was as flamboyant as his paintings and not only painted but created ballets and two short films. He appeared as a guest on television programs including the *Tonight* show with Johnny Carson. With his thin, twirled mustache and often wearing a cape, he was a bigger-than-life character.

With hope in his heart that the painting was genuine, Loughlin took his find to Sotheby's in New York City, where it was authenticated by David Norman, who at that time was a vice-president in the Department of Impressionist and Modern Art. Both Loughlin and Norman were delighted, and the decision was to put the painting up for sale at Sotheby's. The portrait was estimated to bring between $80,000 and $100,000.

When Robert Descharmes, a Dalí expert, looked at the painting, he knew it well. The work, entitled "Portrait of the Marquis de Cuevas," was included in his catalog and had been exhibited in a show of Dalí portraits at the Knoedler Gallery in Manhattan in 1943. How the painting had landed at the back of a thrift shop was a mystery. Sotheby's had checked with the Art Loss Register of the International Foundation for Art Research to make sure it wasn't stolen. It was not.

The painting had an interesting history. According to Norman, the subject of the portrait, the Marquis de Cuevas, was one of the Zodiac Group started in France in 1932. Twelve collectors paid a monthly sum to Dalí, and in return each received one painting a year. The marquis was a cultivated Chilean who ran a dance troupe in the 1920s and 1930s with his wife, Margaret Rockefeller Strong. When the marquis died, the portrait eventually became the property of Margaret Rockefeller Strong's next husband, Raymundo Lorrain.

When the painting of the marquis was auctioned at Sotheby's, November 13, 1996, it sold for $184,000. The proceeds were divided between Loughlin and the beneficiary of the estate of Raymundo Lorrain.

Loughlin said that he had always felt some kind of connection to Dalí because he was a Taurus and so was Dalí. He also owned a belt buckle created by Dalí and had seen him on Johnny Carson's *Tonight* show.

Who knows what future vibrations for finding treasure can be gained from watching television? In any event, what brought Loughlin a treasure was being first in line. Remember what they say about the early bird!

CHAPTER 35

ART McKEE AND THE 1733 FLEET

They call him the granddaddy of treasure hunters because he was one of the first to comb the depths of the ocean, searching for sunken ships. When he began in the 1940s, divers wore heavy helmets and even heavier suits. It was dangerous business, but he loved it. His name is Art McKee.

McKee was born in 1910 and in the 1940s, before he turned to treasure, he was the keeper of the Homestead, Florida, swimming pool. According to treasure hunter and author Bob Weller, McKee bought his first diving helmet at a pawnshop and met a boat captain who showed him the location of a sunken ship. The work of actually finding the treasures of what turned out to be the *Capitana El Rui*, the lead ship of the 1733 fleet, was up to McKee. Before he died in 1980, he had lived his dream and found his treasure.

Just knowing the site of a sunken treasure ship didn't guarantee finding the riches aboard. In those early days many died before they could hold a treasure in their hands. Not only was the seventy-pound helmet cumbersome, but the two-hundred-pound lead weighted suit could easily mean disaster if the diver fell. Air lines from the diver were attached to the equipment on the boat above, and if those lines to the surface tangled, it could also mean the end for the treasure hunter.

Against all odds, McKee persevered and eventually found millions of dollars worth of gold, silver, and jewels. He used a land-mine sweeper that he converted to act as a metal detector, and was really the forerunner of the modern-day metal detectors. He is also credited with adapting and inventing other tools of the trade.

One of his first treasures from the *Capitana El Rui* was a

Art McKee, displaying a huge silver bar recovered from the 1733 fleet.

seventy-five-pound silver bar from the Potosi mines of Bolivia, which was displayed at the Smithsonian Institution. McKee had a love of history and felt the treasure should be shown to the world—so he built his own museum to house his precious finds. It is at the 86.7-mile marker in the Florida Keys, in the area where he first found three of the 1733 fleet ships.

In addition to the treasures of the 1733 fleet, McKee displayed coins and other artifacts he found while working at other locations. One was the pirate stronghold of Port Royal, Jamaica. In 1692 a huge earthquake killed 5,000 and the town disappeared into the sea, covered by 30 feet of water. McKee and others searched for the lost pirate loot.

His daughter Karen McKee kept the museum going and proudly displayed artifacts found by her father. There were emeralds in matrix (the natural state) worth $25,000 and a jewel-encrusted gold pendant worth half a million dollars, in addition to a wide variety of coins and jewelry.

Karen is also an accomplished diver and treasure hunter, and obviously her favorite site is the *Capitana El Rui.* She said that her father first taught her to dive there when she was nine. The wreck is in 21 feet of water with 11 feet of sand covering the huge timbers that are the only remains of the once sleek galleon. Before anyone can search for treasure at the site, the sand must be blown away by using the "mailbox" blowers developed by Mel Fisher.

Two years ago, when Karen's son Terry Ballard was seven, she decided it was time for him to continue the family legacy. He was already trained to dive with scuba equipment but had practiced only in pools. It was an emotional experience for all involved when, for the first time, Terry stood on the bottom of the sea with his mother and then sat on a timber of his grandfather's great discovery, the *Capitana El Rui.*

Three years ago, Joe Shepherd, a teacher from Indiana who was diving on the wreck, found a coin called a "pillar dollar." He was overwhelmed when he learned it was worth $6,000. He proved that one need not be a professional treasure hunter to find riches under the sea.

Professional treasure hunter Joe Kimball is just one of the many who still work the *Capitana El Rui.* He says that $600,000 in treasure has been found there in the past five years, and the grand total from the time McKee made his find is estimated at $100 million.

Kimball says, "The wonderful thing about a treasure wreck is how it can live for so long. We're still finding treasure on it." That would undoubtedly make Art McKee very happy.

CHAPTER 36

HOW TO FIND TREASURE AND WHAT TO DO IF YOU FIND IT

Now that you have read about the amazing treasures people have found accidentally, or by diligent work, you may say, "I can do that," and you can. Obviously you won't be able to duplicate the feats of Mel Fisher and Bob Marx, but remember, Kip Wagner was just walking along the beach when he found coins from the 1715 fleet.

As you now know, people from all over the world have happened upon gold, coins, jewels, documents, furniture, and cars, as well as all sorts of items that didn't seem to be worth anything but turned out to be valuable. To help you get started, we are providing sources for you to contact, whether you want to go metal detecting yourself or think you have found treasure in your attic, garage, living room, or at a swap meet or neighborhood auction. The sky's the limit and, as you've discovered, meteorites can fall right in your own backyard.

You have read that people at the major auction houses are always hoping that someone will call them who has the special item that will prove to be a real treasure. One good point to remember is that if you think something has value, check it out. If it is a document or furniture, the library is a great place to start research. Reference librarians are very helpful, and in most cases are happy to be asked to help. Remember the woman who had the table worth $350,000? When a friend suggested it might be valuable, she went to the library and tried to find pictures of a table like it. Then she got in touch with the people who were expert in American antiques.

If you enjoy going to garage sales, auctions, and swap meets, begin to do some reading on antiques of all kinds. Again, the library is a great place to begin. So many times people pass up something that has great value because they have no idea it is worth anything.

Before providing a list of some auction houses and people who deal in specific items such as movie posters and furniture, we turn to one of the easiest ways you can become a treasure hunter. You can go metal detecting and find everything from gold, through historic items and jewelry, to meteorites.

You needn't run out and buy a detector. Many dealers will rent one to you. This way you can find out if the activity is something you will enjoy. Once people are hooked, they don't want to give it up. Finding that first little coin buried in the sand on the beach, or in a park or other spot, can be a thrill. Hearing the beep of the detector, digging down and actually seeing something there in the ground or sand, is an experience. It's also great exercise, a good way to meet people and even to travel. As Ed Milota, an expert California treasure hunter, says, "When I'm looking for one thing, I always find another. Everything from a septic tank to $48,000 in gold coins buried in the Ojai, California, area." This is the terrific thing about treasure hunting, every beep of the metal detector is a new adventure.

The average cost of metal detectors is about $300, but some are less and others run $900 or more. Some detectors can pick up the reading for a quarter and others can discriminate between junk such as foil and pull tabs and real valuables, and can find objects a foot or more below ground. Most hunters wear earphones to keep the machine sounds from disturbing others.

Metal detecting is great for all ages and is a recreation that can be enjoyed by the entire family. There are many clubs around the United States, and in many cases, parents, children, and grandparents belong.

It is very important to remember that you cannot just go out anywhere with a metal detector. There are strict laws governing where and when you can be a treasure hunter. Digging without permission is not allowed in most parks and other inland property around the country. Careful treasure hunters always replace the earth they dig up. In order to go treasure hunting on private property, you must have permission of the owner and an agreement as to how you will divide what you find. Some federal land has restrictions on any type of metal detecting, so remember, you can't just rush out there and hope for the best.

This is one reason it is a good idea to get in touch with, and even join, a group of treasure-hunting enthusiasts in your area. So that you can find a group near you, or one that you can contact if there isn't a club nearby, we have listed a national organization that has 138 groups around the country and more than 5,000 members. The members of the various groups have varied interests, not only in gold and silver underground. They can also help you if you want to pan for gold in rivers and streams, which requires equipment other than metal detectors. You should contact:

The Federation of Metal Detector and Archaeological Clubs, 5043 Strasbourg Way, Sacramento, California 95842. Phone: (916) 331–7931; fax: *51. (Dues: $5 per year.)

White Electronics (for metal detectors): (800) 547–6911.

They will provide a great deal of information without pushing you to purchase a metal detector.

You read about Jimmy Sierra and the Goat Doctor treasure. Each summer Sierra conducts tours to England that are very popular. He can be reached at Jimmy Sierra Discovery Tours: (415) 457–2910.

Fisher Research Laboratories (for metal detectors), Los Banos, California. Phone: (209) 826–3292.

Garrett Metal Detectors: (800) 527–4011.

If you think you've found a meteorite or want to know more about this, you can contact:

Meteorite Man, Robert A. Haag, P.O. Box 27527, Tucson, Arizona 85726. Phone: (520) 882–8804; fax: (520) 743–7225. E-mail: bobhaag@primenet.com. Haag invites you to visit his Web site for the latest and best meteorite deals in the galaxy, www.meteoriteman.com. If you send a sample, you must include phone number and return postage or it will be discarded.

If you want to go dinosaur hunting or think you might have found part of one, contact:

Black Hills Institute of Geological Research, Inc., P.O. Box 643, 217 Main Street, Hill City, South Dakota 57745. Phone: (605) 574–4289.

Now we turn to the other treasures you find without a metal detector. You have read about the people who found a variety of items, from the Civil War coat to movie posters. There are sources you can get in touch with if you want to know more about specific items.

Civil War enthusiasts can contact:

The Union Drummer Boy, 34 York Street (just off the square), Gettysburg, Pennsylvania 17325. Phone: (717) 334–2350. The store owners can provide a wealth of information for people wanting to pursue this interest.

Don Troiani, P.O. Box 660, Southbury, Connecticut 06488. Phone: (203) 262–6560; fax: (203) 262–6979. Web site: www.dontroiani.com. He is a valuable source of information on both the Revolutionary War and the Civil War.

Those of you who want to find gems can contact:

Gem Mountain, Highway 226, P.O. Box 488, Spruce Pine, North Carolina 28777. Phone: (888) 817–5829 *or* (828) 765–6130. Visit their Web site: www.gemmountain.com. You can order buckets of rocks and find your treasure at home if you can't visit the mine.

Crater of Diamonds State Park, Route 1, Box 364, Murfreesboro, Arkansas 71958. Phone: (870) 285–3113. If you want to find a diamond, this is the place.

Gems of Pala, P.O. Box 382, Pala, California 92059. Phone: (760) 742–1356. If you have a yen for tourmalines, you can purchase buckets of rocks from the mine when visiting in the area. Call for times when they are open.

Aviation enthusiasts:

The Lost Squadron Hangar (Museum) at the airport in Middlesboro, Kentucky. Mailing address: P.O. Box 776, Middlesboro, Kentucky 40965. Phone: (606) 248–1149.

As noted in the opening, the best place to start doing research on the items that appeal to you is the library. An interesting reference source there is the *Encyclopedia of Associations,* which lists many organizations for collectors. You could find a group devoted to an item you particularly like and, by contacting them, learn a great deal about its value. People who collect thimbles have found some that are worth $5,000. Most things that can be collected turn out to be treasures when the rare item is found.

You may not find movie posters in your walls but might

happen upon some in other locations. If you want to sell posters contact:

Dwight Cleveland, P.O. Box 10922, Chicago, Illinois 60610–0922. Phone: (773) 525–9152; fax: (773) 525–2969.

You have read about the amazing treasures that were sold by the noted auction houses and you can get in touch with any or all of the following companies if you think you have found an item of value. Call first and ask for the proper department. Sotheby's, Christie's, and Butterfield & Butterfield handle quite a variety of items such as furniture, paintings, documents, books, movie memorabilia, jewelry, china, and, in the case of Butterfield's, guns and armaments.

Sotheby's, 1334 York Avenue, New York, New York 10021. Phone: (212) 606–7000.

Christie's, 20 Rockefeller Plaza, New York, New York 10020. Phone: (212) 636–2000; fax: (212) 752–3956.

Butterfield & Butterfield, 7601 Sunset Boulevard, Los Angeles, California 90046. Phone: (323) 850–7500; fax: (323) 850–5843. In San Francisco, 220 San Bruno Avenue, San Francisco, California 94103. Phone: (415) 861–7500; fax: (415) 861–8951. For armaments, specifically contact Greg Martin in the San Francisco office.

Israel Sack, Inc., 730 Fifth Avenue, Suite 605, New York, New York 10019. Phone: (212) 399–6562; fax: (212) 399–9252. This is the premier company in the world dealing with American antiques. According to Sack, American antiques are now the most expensive in the world. Sack has sold items recently for well over $1 million. That is the amount paid for just one table or chair, so pay attention to things you see at garage sales or swap meets. Don't forget to look at your furniture and that of friends and neighbors; you could have a treasure in your midst.

If you want to have an item appraised before contacting auction houses or other dealers, you can contact:

American Society of Appraisers in New York City and be referred to an appraiser in your area. Phone (212) 687–6305 or Phone: (800) ASAVALU.

Antiquarian Booksellers, 20 W. 44th Street, New York, New York 10036. Phone: (212) 757–9395. They can provide information on rare and valuable books.

Charles Sachs, The Scriptorium, P.O. Box 1290, Beverly Hills, California 90213. Phone: (310) 275–6060. Expert on historic manuscripts and items of popular culture.

Now that you have sources to help you become an informed treasure hunter, it's time to go to it. We wish you good luck and happy hunting. Remember Mel Fisher's motto: "Today's the day!"

PHOTO CREDITS FOR *THE HUNT FOR AMAZING TREASURES*

The following images are courtesy of:

1. Page from *The Adventures of Huckleberry Finn*, Buffalo and Erie County Public Library
2. Bob Marx and the *Maravilla*, Robert F. Marx
3. Assyrian panel, © Christie's Images, London
4. Jimmy Normandi holding coins, James A. Normandi
5. Jerry Murphy and *El Cazador*, photo of Captain Jerry Murphy taken by Deborah Hale
6. House with posters, picture courtesy of Andrew Solt Productions
7. Sandy Perceval and cigars, photographer, Serena Perceval
8. Declaration of Independence, Rare Books Division, The New York Public Library, Astor, Lenox and Tilden Foundations
9. The Maltese Falcon, from the collection of Dr. Gary Milan. Maltese Falcon from the 1941 Warner Bros./Turner Entertainment Co. motion picture
10. Items from Steamboat *Arabia, Arabia* Steamboat Museum, Kansas City, Missouri
11. Washington's inaugural, Phillips Auctioneers, London

12. Hoxne Hoard, photo taken by Suffolk County Council Archaeological Service
13. Cover of *Tamerlane*, courtesy of the 19th Century Shop, Baltimore
14. Cole Younger gun, Butterfield and Butterfield
15. Roosevelt ring, Franklin D. Roosevelt Library
16. Kay Modgling, picture courtesy of Andrew Solt Productions
17. Head of *T. rex*, The Field Museum, Chicago, Illinois
18. Mojave Nugget, courtesy of Wayne C. Leicht, photo taken by Harold and Erica Van Pelt
19. Amarillo Starlight Diamond, Crater of Diamonds State Park, Murfreesboro, Arkansas
20. The Punch Jones Diamond, photo taken by Arnout Hyde, Jr.
21. Mel Fisher and *Atocha* treasure, Mel Fisher photo courtesy of Pat Clyne
22. Treasure from 1715 fleet, photo taken by Daniel C. Wagner
23. Charles Buchanan of Gem Mountain, Charles Buchanan
24. The Rembrandt plate, © Christie's Images, London
25. The Goddard–Townsend table, Albert M. Sack
26. Robert Haag, Meteorite Man, photo taken by Fotosmith-Jeff Smith
27. Blue Sheppard of Gems of Pala, J. Blue Sheppard
28. Bob and Margaret Weller, © Allen Eyestone/*The Palm Beach Post*
29. Storage locker, Federal Bureau of Investigation
30. Oldest Levi's, Ron Hamilton
31. The So-Cal Belly Tank (race car), Bruce Meyer
32. P-38 from Lost Squadron, Photo, Lou Sapienza
33. Civil War coat, Don Troiani
34. Salvador Dalí painting, © 1999 Artists Rights Society (ARS), New York
35. Art McKee (with silver bullion), photo taken by Daniel C. Wagner